The Great Minnesota
COOKIE BOOK

The Great Minnesota
COOKIE BOOK

Award-Winning Recipes from the
Star Tribune's Holiday Cookie Contest

Lee Svitak Dean and Rick Nelson

Photography by Tom Wallace

University of Minnesota Press

Minneapolis/London

Published by the University of Minnesota Press
111 Third Avenue South, Suite 290
Minneapolis, MN 55401-2520
http://www.upress.umn.edu

Book design by bedesign, inc.

Printed in China on acid-free paper

The University of Minnesota is an equal-opportunity educator and employer.

24 23 22 21 20 19   10 9 8 7 6 5 4 3

Library of Congress Cataloging-in-Publication Data
Dean, Lee Svitak, author. | Nelson, Rick, author. |
    Wallace, Tom (Photographer).
The great Minnesota cookie book : award-winning recipes from the Star
    Tribune's holiday cookie contest / Lee Svitak Dean and Rick Nelson ;
    photography by Tom Wallace.
Minneapolis : University of Minnesota Press, [2018] | Includes index.
Identifiers: LCCN 2018008934 | ISBN 978-1-5179-0583-5 (lithocase)
Subjects: LCSH: Cookies. | Holiday cooking—Minnesota. | LCGFT: Cookbooks.
Classification: LCC TX772 .D42 2018 | DDC 641.86/5409776—dc23
LC record available at https://lccn.loc.gov/2018008934

In flour-dusted gratitude for the many bakers
who put the merry into sweet treats

CONTENTS

Introduction

Fifteen years ago, Rick Nelson offered a simple suggestion that was to change our holiday planning for years to come in the Taste food section of the *Star Tribune*: "Let's have a cookie contest."

Sounds simple enough: select the best cookie from a pile of entries. How difficult can that be?

Well, more than 3,500 recipes later, we can say that it's not only a lot of work—both in the office and in the kitchen—but the contest has become our own beloved holiday tradition, one that has left a trail of flour dust, toasted almonds, and bits of chocolate along the way. The delicious results from all those winning cookies are in your hands: the best recipes from fifteen years of the *Star Tribune*'s Holiday Cookie Contest.

It's an event that sends many local bakers to the kitchen year-round to experiment and fine-tune their recipes, in hopes of winning the coveted designation as top cookie of the season, which inevitably results in sold-out specialty ingredients in local supermarkets. There was the run on almond flour one year, and on sliced almonds and pistachios during others, that resulted in frenzied bakers in search of the season's must-have item.

This comes as no surprise to us, given the baking culture of the state—all those cold days and nights to fill and, historically, a heritage with a fondness for baked goods (thank the Scandinavians and Germans). Not so incidentally, Minnesota is the home of a butter cooperative and flour companies. The Mississippi River's St. Anthony Falls powered the wheat mills. And we have a state muffin—blueberry! Let us not forget that the granddaddy of all baking contests, the Pillsbury Bake-Off, was born in Minneapolis.

So, yes, baking is in our DNA.

Our prep starts in mid-September as we post the announcements for the competition. Over the next four weeks, entries trickle in, until days before the deadline when there's a barrage of recipes that suddenly appear. Readers aren't much different from reporters—we all need deadlines!

Minutes after the clock strikes noon—always the cutoff time—we begin to sift through the stack of recipes, some handwritten in the careful script of a baker of many years, most of them printed from a computer. The entries arrive from all sorts of kitchens: from teachers representing their classrooms, from bakers in their twenties or in their eighties, and, once, from an inmate at the county jail. Many participants offer the story behind their cookie, poignant tales of the link between past and present that so often revolve around the dinner table.

It all begins with the recipe. The stack of two hundred to three hundred recipes awaits as we try to figure out, one by one, which will taste better than the next. For the first cut, based on our longtime experience of reading recipes, we simply use our eyes to gauge which cookies have the most appeal as we sort them into piles of "must have," "possible," and "not a chance."

Though the entries don't need to be created specifically for our contest, we look for cookies that will be new to most bakers—new being relative, of course. Sometimes those are heirloom recipes that have been in families for generations; occasionally the contenders are familiar favorites that have been tweaked by bakers. Original cookies find their way into the mix, developed by contestants who tap into current food trends (think sea salt, espresso, and brown butter—and, yes, even kale).

Spritz, cornflake wreaths, and snickerdoodles won't make the cut, though they are longtime favorites of many. The operative word is "favorites." We are not looking for recipes that everyone already has—this contest calls for something different. The recipes that make the winner's circle must delight and inspire both longtime bakers and those entering the kitchen for the first time.

Each year, the selected finalists need to represent not only a breadth of flavors and textures for the home baker (we can't present all chocolate or all sandwich cookies, for example), but also a variety in appearance, since the winning treats are published as the winter holidays begin, a time when bakers are prepping for festive cookie platters. We also keep in mind winners of the past because we want to avoid overlap.

First we narrow the number of entries to the best-sounding twenty to thirty recipes. Truth be told, we have our own particular likes and dislikes that we tap into as we go through the possibilities; no cake-mix cookies ever make it to the testing pile, and we're not big on cereal additions either. Then we call on our stable of very reliable bakers to prepare the recipes and join us at the judging table. For many years, these were *Star Tribune* colleagues. More recently, we shifted to the skills of a pastry chef and her crew to prepare the cookies for a team of judges that includes prior contest winners and other accomplished bakers.

We begin the marathon sampling with a warning, based on our years of judging food contests: "Pace yourself. You don't have to eat the entire cookie." Milk and water are in ready supply as palate cleansers for the tasters who will face more cookies in an hour than most would otherwise eat in a month. During the contest's fifteen years, our judges have sampled more than 325 varieties. We won't even begin to consider the calorie count.

As the judges sit at the table, the sheets of cookies, in all their grandeur, offer an initial thrill, a buffet of treats that shout "special occasion." Then reality sets in. We each nibble a corner of the first recipe. "Too many ingredients," mumbles one judge. "What am I supposed to be tasting?" Murmurs of agreement sound off around the table.

The next cookie makes the rounds. "The chocolate is nice, but the texture is off," notes a critic. "This is way too savory for a cookie," says another. And on it goes, one by one, as the rejects pile up on overflowing paper plates, until one cookie catches our notice.

"I love this lemon flavor," says a judge with a smile. "This is a keeper."

Is the cookie too sweet or too difficult to make? Are the ingredients readily available? Is it too ordinary, or does it belong on a holiday platter? Has a similar cookie been a contender in the past? Is a bar really a cookie? (We think so.) These are the questions we ask as we sample the entries.

The finalists generally become apparent quickly. You can tell because the judges take a second bite. Determining the winner often takes a bit longer, with plenty of discussion, compromise, and banter among the judges—polite, of course; we are Minnesotans, after all.

One year we videotaped a session, thinking it would be of interest to readers to see how one cookie was chosen over another. Then, as the judges delivered their commentary with brutal honesty (they were there to pick a winner, after all), we recognized that, sometimes, it's better not to hear what others think of your recipe.

• • • •

A skeptic may wonder how many new cookie recipes there can be. After all, the ingredients tend to be the same basic four: flour, butter, sugar, and eggs.

That's just the beginning, of course. It's the cinnamon and cardamom, the almond paste and coconut, citrus and, of course, chocolate (semisweet or dark) and nuts (pecan, walnut, pistachio, hazelnut, almond, cashew, peanut, and macadamia) in all their delightful variations that transform the ordinary into the extraordinary bite of perfection.

In the end, perhaps there is nothing simple about the cookie. Nothing, that is, except for its goodness. But don't take our word for it. Head to the kitchen and give these winners a try. Your cookie platter is waiting, and we have seventy-nine recipes for you to bake.

Cookie
MEMORIES

A Cookie by Many Names

Lee Svitak Dean

When I think of Russian tea cakes, I remember the week of making seven hundred cookies. Yes, I was crazed, even by my own standards. Big events do that to me.

The occasion was my daughter's senior art show at her college in Iowa. It was December and she needed a holiday-themed spread of goodies to serve during the opening reception for the hungry crowd of students, faculty, friends, and family who would descend on her exhibit.

A week before the gathering, after the dinner dishes were finished, I reached for the worn *Betty Crocker's Cooky Book* (yes, that's the way Betty spelled it) and baked for seven nights in a row, one hundred cookies at a time. At the end of that baking frenzy, I packed up the tins and Tupperware to be transported through snowy cornfields along the two-lane highway to Luther College.

I baked other cookies for the reception, of course. Even I wouldn't make seven hundred Russian tea cakes. But those I remember, probably because they are a favorite of mine. The little mounds of powdered sugar that look like snowballs have been on every family holiday cookie plate for as long as I can remember, whether it was at Grandma Nelson's house or Auntie Joan's or my mother's.

December was the only time I saw the cookies, which may be part of their appeal. Those treats are wrapped in fond memories of the hustle and bustle, warm hugs and crisp air that surrounded us as one relative after another opened the front door, stomped off the snow, and settled into our merrymaking.

It was not only the cookies' holiday appearance that prompts me to grab one mound, then another. The tea cakes aren't very sweet, which is my preference in a cookie. The dominant flavors are butter and ground nuts . . . and powdered sugar. Lots of powdered sugar. These may be the only cookies that need a warning: do not inhale while eating (that powdered sugar dust can be dangerous!)—and definitely don't eat while wearing black.

Then there is the name, which enchants me. Or, shall we say, the many names for the cookie: Russian tea cakes, Mexican wedding cakes, pecan sandies, pecan butter balls, and butter balls.

The first Mexican wedding cake recipe doesn't turn up in cookbooks until the 1950s, though its heritage clearly extends back generations, if not centuries, perhaps in part because the cookies are so durable—they travel well and can be kept for a long time. At my grandmother's house, they were packed in tins weeks before the holidays arrived and stored on the cold stairs that led to the attic.

The cookies probably date back to medieval Arab cuisine, where even then they were saved for special occasions and made of what would have been expensive ingredients at the time—butter, sugar, and nuts. The treats were brought by the Moors to Spain, where they are called *polvorones* (based on the Spanish word for dust, *polvo*). Like any good food, they spread across Europe and eventually crossed the ocean, where they traveled across the New World and to Mexico and beyond.

Whether made of pecans, almonds, or hazelnuts—or cashews in the Philippines, macadamias in Hawaii—the nutty treats belong at the world table. And at my table, as well. But this year I'll stick to a single batch.

RUSSIAN TEA CAKES

MAKES ABOUT 4 DOZEN COOKIES

Note: This dough must be prepared in advance. Pecans are traditionally in these cookies in the United States, though any nut could be substituted. Want to change up the recipe? Try making them with macadamia nuts. This version comes from the 1963 *Betty Crocker's Cooky Book*. A photograph in that book shows a variation of these cookies rolled in colored sprinkles instead of powdered sugar, but somehow that seems wrong.

2¼ cups flour
¼ teaspoon salt
1 cup (2 sticks) unsalted butter, at room temperature

½ cup powdered sugar, plus more for rolling
1 teaspoon vanilla extract
¾ cup finely chopped nuts, such as pecans

In a small bowl, whisk together the flour and salt, and reserve. In a bowl of an electric mixer on medium-high speed, beat the butter until creamy, about 1 minute. Reduce the speed to low, add ½ cup powdered sugar and vanilla extract, and mix until combined. Increase the speed to medium-high and beat until light and fluffy, about 2 minutes. Reduce the speed to low, add the flour mixture, and mix until thoroughly combined. Stir in the nuts. Cover the bowl in plastic wrap and refrigerate at least 2 hours, or overnight.

When ready to bake, preheat the oven to 400°F and line the baking sheets with parchment paper. Shape the dough into 1-inch balls and place 1 inch apart on the prepared baking sheets (the cookies do not spread). Bake until set but not brown, 10 to 12 minutes. Remove the cookies from the oven and cool 5 minutes. While the cookies are still warm, carefully roll them in powdered sugar. Transfer the cookies to a wire rack to cool; then roll them in powdered sugar again.

The Ultimate Cookie Pairing

Rick Nelson

When I was growing up, my father's extended family gathered on Christmas Eve for an enormous, controlled-pandemonium celebration. My dad or one of his brothers would gamely pull on an ill-fitting Santa suit (their wingtips always gave them up as suburban stand-ins for the real St. Nick), and my mom and aunts would prepare an enormous buffet potluck supper. Dessert was invariably lefse and cookies, and I quickly learned to gravitate toward the platter prepared by Aunt Marge Hermstad, a woman who definitely knows her way around flour, eggs, butter, and sugar.

We're talking about the late 1960s here, so forgive my cobwebbed memory, but I can recall ignoring julekake, toffee bars, date balls, and other goodies in favor of what my preadolescent brain decided was the cookie embodiment of the True Meaning of Christmas. In other words, Marge's Peanut Butter Chocolate Kiss Cookies.

Their allure? Simple. An entire Hershey's Kiss, a wildly extravagant culinary gesture.

The cookie itself, a tender, crackle-topped peanut butter treat, was a big draw too, particularly since I practically lived on peanut butter (and, truth to tell, still do).

Now, all these years later, I continue to nurture a not-so-secret crush on the cookie also known as the Peanut Blossom, a Pillsbury Bake-Off winner from 1957. I've always enjoyed baking them too. They come together in a snap, and they routinely elicit an "Oh, my favorite," a phrase that bakers everywhere never tire of hearing.

Through trial and error, I've discovered that the secret to Peanut Blossom success is to forgo the Jif–Skippy universe in favor of an all-natural peanut butter. I don't even mind the tedious task of extricating all of those Kisses from their foil wrappers, probably because it's an unwritten requirement that the cook sneak a few. Okay, more than a few.

When we met for lunch last summer, Aunt Marge, true to form, arrived with a gift from her kitchen: a plastic container filled with brownies. Treasure, truly. They were delicious. If I were the thoughtful nephew she deserves, I'd replenish that Tupperware with Peanut Butter Chocolate Kiss Cookies and get it over to her house, pronto. I'd better get baking.

PEANUT BUTTER CHOCOLATE KISS COOKIES
MAKES ABOUT 3 DOZEN COOKIES

Note: This dough must be prepared in advance. Adapted from *A Baker's Field Guide to Christmas Cookies*, by Dede Wilson.

1¼ cups flour

1 teaspoon baking soda

½ teaspoon salt

½ cup (1 stick) unsalted butter, at room temperature

1 cup smooth, unsalted, natural (not hydrogenated) peanut butter

½ cup granulated sugar, plus more for coating

½ cup firmly packed light brown sugar

½ teaspoon vanilla extract

1 egg

36 milk chocolate kisses, unwrapped

In a medium bowl, whisk together the flour, baking soda, and salt, and reserve.

In a bowl of an electric mixer on medium-high speed, beat the butter and peanut butter together until creamy, about 2 minutes. Add ½ cup granulated sugar and light brown sugar, and beat until light and fluffy, about 3 minutes. Add the vanilla extract and egg, and mix until fully combined. Reduce the speed to low. Add one-third of the flour mixture and mix until just combined. Gradually add the remaining flour, mixing until just blended.

Scrape the dough onto a large piece of plastic wrap. Use the wrap to help shape the dough into a large, flat disk; then cover it completely with wrap. Refrigerate until the dough is firm enough to roll into balls, at least 1 hour or overnight.

When ready to bake, preheat the oven to 350°F and line the baking sheets with parchment paper. Shape the dough into 1½-inch balls. Roll the dough balls in granulated sugar, coating them completely, and place 2 inches apart on the prepared baking sheets. Gently flatten the dough balls just enough so they don't roll off the baking sheets. Bake just until light golden brown on bottoms, about 16 to 18 minutes; do not overbake. Remove from the oven, gently press a chocolate kiss into the center of each cookie (cookies may crack; that's okay), and return the cookies to the oven for 1 minute. Remove from the oven and cool for 2 minutes before transferring the cookies to a wire rack to cool completely.

Cookie
WISDOM

Tips for Great Cookies

Delicious cookies are just eight easy-to-follow tips away.

1. Prepare yourself. Before beginning, read the recipe from start to finish, twice.

2. Shop with this list. The cookie recipes in this book call for large eggs, all-purpose flour, and unsalted butter, unless otherwise noted. For optimum results, invest in fresh baking powder, baking soda, and spices. Shop in the bulk section for spices: you'll save money by purchasing only what you need, and the flavors are generally more potent.

3. Equip your kitchen. Use flat, shiny, and rimless medium- to heavy-gauge aluminum baking sheets. Skip the nonstick and use (and reuse) parchment paper or silicon (such as Silpat) baking mats.

4. Measure carefully. Spoon flour and powdered sugar into the measuring cup (rather than use the measuring cup as a scoop), and level ingredients with a straightedge, such as a knife. Butter is at room temperature when a light touch leaves a slight indentation, about 30 to 45 minutes outside the refrigerator.

5. Reach for the spatula. When mixing dough, take a moment to scrape the bottom and sides of the bowl, and then resume mixing.

6. Stay in shape. To keep round refrigerator cookies from going flat, place the logs wrapped in plastic or wax paper on a level shelf in the refrigerator and give the dough a quarter-turn every 15 minutes for the first hour in the refrigerator.

7. Bake evenly. Preheat the oven for at least 20 minutes. Adjust the baking rack to the oven's middle position. For true accuracy, invest in an oven thermometer; Target, amazon.com, and other major retailers sell a reliable model for about seven dollars, an expenditure that will more than likely pay for itself. If the recipe includes a range of baking times, begin by setting the timer for the least amount of time. Place one baking sheet at a time in the oven, rotating it halfway through the baking time. Cool the baking sheets completely between batches by alternating among several baking sheets or by running hot ones under cold water. Heat can cause dough to spread.

8. Store wisely. Most cookies remain fresh for up to a week when stored in an airtight container at room temperature. Store different cookies in separate containers. Freeze cookies undecorated. When ready to serve, thaw and decorate.

Drop
COOKIES

CANDY CANE SUGAR COOKIES
MAKES ABOUT 4 DOZEN COOKIES

Note: When smashing the peppermint candy, consider using a paper or plastic bag, or lining the top of the cutting board with parchment or wax paper, and covering the candy too.

For cookies:

2½	cups flour	1¼	cups granulated sugar
1	teaspoon baking soda	3	egg yolks
½	teaspoon cream of tartar	1	teaspoon vanilla extract
¼	teaspoon salt	1	teaspoon peppermint extract
1	cup (2 sticks) unsalted butter, at room temperature	1	cup (about 6 ounces) crushed candy canes or peppermint hard candies

For icing:

½	cup (1 stick) unsalted butter, at room temperature	2	cups powdered sugar
4	ounces cream cheese, at room temperature	⅛	teaspoon salt
1	teaspoon peppermint extract	2	drops red food coloring

To prepare cookies: Preheat the oven to 350°F and line the baking sheets with parchment paper. In a large bowl, whisk together the flour, baking soda, cream of tartar, and salt, and reserve.

In a bowl of an electric mixer on medium-high speed, beat the butter until creamy, about 1 minute. Add the granulated sugar, and beat until light and fluffy, about 2 minutes. Add the egg yolks, one at a time, beating well after each addition. Add the vanilla extract and peppermint extract, and beat until well combined. Reduce the speed to low, add the flour mixture, and mix until just combined. Stir in the candy pieces.

Drop tablespoons of the dough 2 inches apart on the prepared baking sheets and bake until tops are cracked and lightly browned, about 11 to 13 minutes. Remove the cookies from the oven and cool for 2 minutes before transferring them to a wire rack to cool completely.

To prepare icing: In a bowl of an electric mixer on medium speed, combine the butter, cream cheese, and peppermint extract, and beat until creamy. Reduce the speed to low, add the powdered sugar and salt, and mix until creamy. Add the food coloring, 1 drop at a time, to reach desired color. Ice cookies.

When Michelle Mazzara of Eagan, Minnesota, was creating this recipe, she kept returning to her Italian grandmother for inspiration. "She was happiest when she was cooking," said Mazzara. "She would bake for two or three months before Christmas, and she would give boxes and boxes of cookies to everyone she knew." Which explains why Mazzara started with Grandma Rose's sugar cookie recipe. "They just sort of melted in your mouth," she said. As for the minty fresh flourish: "The scent of peppermint is very vivid in my mind when I think about Christmas," Mazzara said.

CHOCOLATE DECADENCE COOKIES
MAKES ABOUT 2 DOZEN COOKIES

Note: The amounts of flour and bittersweet chocolate are correctly indicated here. For added flavor, we toasted the walnuts. To toast walnuts, place the nuts in a dry skillet over medium heat and cook, stirring (or shaking the pan frequently), until they just begin to release their fragrance, about 3 to 4 minutes (alternately, preheat oven to 325°F, spread the nuts on an ungreased baking sheet, and bake, stirring often, for 4 to 6 minutes). Remove the nuts from the heat and cool to room temperature.

2 **eggs**	8 **ounces bittersweet chocolate, coarsely chopped (such as Ghirardelli's 60 percent cacao bittersweet chocolate)**
½ **cup granulated sugar**	
1 **teaspoon vanilla extract**	
¼ **cup flour**	2 **tablespoons unsalted butter**
¼ **teaspoon baking powder**	1½ **cups coarsely chopped walnuts or other nuts (toasted, if desired)**
⅛ **teaspoon salt**	
	6 **ounces semisweet chocolate chips**

Preheat the oven to 350°F and line the baking sheets with parchment paper. In a small bowl, whisk together the eggs, granulated sugar, and vanilla extract. Set the bowl in a larger bowl of hot tap water.

In a small bowl, whisk together the flour, baking powder, and salt, and reserve.

In a double boiler over gently simmering water (or in a bowl in a microwave oven), combine the bittersweet chocolate and butter, and stir until melted and smooth. Remove from heat and stir in the egg mixture until thoroughly combined. Stir in the flour mixture. Stir in the walnuts and chocolate chips.

Drop slightly rounded tablespoons of the dough 2 inches apart on the prepared baking sheets and bake until the surface looks dry and the centers are still gooey, about 10 minutes. Do not overbake. Remove the cookies from the oven and cool for 2 minutes before transferring them to a wire rack to cool completely.

"This is the first contest I've ever entered," said Elaine Prebonich of New Brighton, Minnesota. "I love to bake. I'm retired. I have the time." She found the recipe in the newspaper "oh, my goodness, maybe fifteen or twenty years ago, and then I've been tweaking it along the way," she said. "It's an absolute favorite, every time I make it." Judges agreed. "'Decadence' is right," was one comment. "Every cookie tray needs chocolate, and these sure pack a chocolate wallop," was another.

CHOCOLATE-DIPPED TRIPLE COCONUT HAYSTACKS

MAKES ABOUT 2 DOZEN COOKIES

Note: For extra flavor to these wheat-free cookies, add lightly roasted, roughly chopped macadamia nuts (about ¾ cup) into the final coconut mixture, dropping the cookies into mounds rather than forming haystacks. You can find unsweetened, desiccated (dried) flaked coconut at most natural foods co-ops.

1 cup coconut milk (not cream of coconut)	½ teaspoon salt
¼ cup granulated sugar	3 cups unsweetened, shredded, desiccated (dried) coconut
2 tablespoons light corn syrup	
4 egg whites	3 cups sweetened flaked or shredded coconut
2 teaspoons vanilla extract	14 ounces semisweet chocolate

Preheat the oven to 375°F and line the baking sheets with parchment paper. In a medium bowl, whisk together the coconut milk, granulated sugar, corn syrup, egg whites, vanilla extract, and salt. In a large bowl, combine the unsweetened and sweetened coconut, breaking apart any lumps. Pour the coconut milk mixture into the coconut, and mix until the coconut is evenly moistened. Refrigerate for 15 minutes.

Drop heaping tablespoons of the dough 1 inch apart on the prepared baking sheets. Form the cookies into four-sided haystacks, moistening your fingers with water if necessary. Bake until light-golden brown, about 15 minutes. Remove the cookies from the oven and cool for 2 minutes before transferring them to a wire rack to cool completely.

In a double boiler over gently simmering water (or in a bowl in a microwave oven), melt the chocolate, stirring occasionally until smooth. Place the wire racks over wax paper.

Holding a cooled cookie by its pointed top, carefully dip the bottom of the haystack into melted chocolate, covering up to one-third of the sides of the cookie. Use chopsticks or a fork to remove the cookie, draining off excess chocolate. Place the cookies, chocolate-side down, on the prepared wire racks. Refrigerate until the chocolate sets, about 30 minutes.

Ron Traxinger of St. Louis Park, Minnesota, doesn't like to follow recipes. "I'll try it once, and then I'll change it," he said. He ran across a recipe for coconut haystacks in a magazine and, true to form, immediately began to tinker with it. The result? An attention-grabber. "When you put them on a platter with other cookies, they're the first ones to go," he said. "They're elegant and sexy. People want to touch them. They're a better version of any macaroon you've tasted in the past." Most of the batches of haystacks that Traxinger prepares will end up as gifts. "But not for the office," he said with a laugh. "They're too good for the office."

CHOCOLATE TOFFEE COOKIES
MAKES ABOUT 4 DOZEN COOKIES

Note: This dough must be prepared in advance. To toast walnuts, place the nuts in a dry skillet over medium heat and cook, stirring (or shaking the pan frequently), until they just begin to release their fragrance, about 3 to 4 minutes (alternately, preheat oven to 325°F, spread the nuts on an ungreased baking sheet, and bake, stirring often, for 4 to 6 minutes). It may seem unusual, but the amounts of flour and vanilla extract are correctly indicated here. And, although the salt is optional, it does create a salty-and-sweet taste that is just a bit different on your cookie plate.

½ cup flour

1 teaspoon baking powder

½ teaspoon salt

1 pound bittersweet or semisweet chocolate, chopped

4 tablespoons (½ stick) unsalted butter

1¾ cup packed brown sugar

4 eggs

1 tablespoon vanilla extract

5 (1.4 ounce) chocolate-covered English toffee bars (such as Heath), coarsely chopped, or 7 ounces Heath bits

1 cup chopped walnuts, toasted

Flaky sea salt for sprinkling, optional

In a medium bowl, whisk together the flour, baking powder, and salt, and reserve. In a double boiler over gently simmering water (or in a bowl in a microwave oven), combine the chocolate and butter, stirring occasionally, until melted and smooth. Remove from heat and cool until the mixture is lukewarm.

In a bowl of an electric mixer on medium speed, beat the brown sugar and eggs until thick, about 5 minutes. Reduce the speed to low, add the chocolate mixture and vanilla extract, and mix until well combined. Add the flour mixture and mix until just combined. Stir in the toffee and walnuts. Cover with plastic wrap and refrigerate for 30 minutes.

When ready to bake, preheat the oven to 350°F and line the baking sheets with parchment paper. Drop heaping tablespoons of the dough 2 inches apart on the prepared baking sheets. Sprinkle each cookie with a pinch of sea salt, if desired. Bake until the tops of the cookies are dry and cracked but are still soft to the touch, about 12 to 14 minutes; do not overbake. Remove the cookies from the oven and cool for 2 minutes before transferring to a wire rack to cool completely.

"I loved Heath bars when I was growing up," said Bonnie Coffey of Pequot Lakes, Minnesota. "Normally, when I look at a cookie recipe, I look at the ratios of fat, flour, and eggs. But this one? It was the toffee component and all of that bittersweet chocolate." She's also a fan of Deb Perelman's Smitten Kitchen blog (smittenkitchen.com), and that's where she first encountered this *Bon Appétit* magazine recipe. "People like chocolate," she said. "It's always going to be a home run."

DEVIL'S DELIGHT COOKIES

MAKES ABOUT 2 DOZEN COOKIES

Note: This recipe calls for chocolate bars infused with cinnamon and red chile, such as Vosges Red Fire chocolate bars (vosgeschocolate.com).

For dusting:

4 teaspoons granulated sugar

4 teaspoons ground cinnamon

⅛ teaspoon cayenne pepper

....

For cookies:

10 ounces bittersweet chocolate, chopped

½ cup plus 2 teaspoons flour

3 tablespoons unsweetened cocoa powder

¼ teaspoon baking powder

¼ teaspoon cayenne pepper

¼ teaspoon salt

5 tablespoons unsalted butter,
    at room temperature

1 cup plus 1 tablespoon granulated sugar

3 eggs

2 teaspoons vanilla extract

3 ounces chocolate bar with cinnamon
    and red chile, chopped

½ cup (3 ounces) cinnamon chips

To prepare dusting: In a small bowl, whisk together the granulated sugar, cinnamon, and cayenne pepper, and reserve.

To prepare cookies: Preheat the oven to 350°F and line the baking sheets with parchment paper. In a double boiler over gently simmering water (or in a bowl in a microwave oven), melt the bittersweet chocolate, stirring until smooth. Remove from heat and cool for 10 minutes.

In a medium bowl, whisk together the flour, cocoa powder, baking powder, cayenne pepper, and salt, and reserve. In a bowl of an electric mixer on medium-high speed, beat the butter until creamy, about 1 minute. Add the granulated sugar and beat until light and fluffy, about 2 minutes. Add the eggs, one at a time, beating well after each addition. Continue to beat until the mixture is pale, light, and creamy, about 5 minutes. Reduce the speed to low, add the lukewarm melted chocolate and vanilla extract, and mix until just combined. Using a spatula, fold in the flour mixture, and then fold in the chopped cinnamon–chile chocolate bar and cinnamon chips.

Drop ¼ cupfuls of the dough 2 inches apart onto the prepared baking sheets. Sprinkle a pinch of dusting mixture over each cookie, and bake until the tops are evenly cracked but the cookies are not yet firm to the touch, about 16 minutes. Remove the cookies from the oven and cool them completely on the baking sheets.

Michelle Clark's minor obsession with a dark chocolate–chipotle truffle got her thinking: could it translate into a cookie? The St. Paul, Minnesota, resident kicked the idea around for a few weeks before formulating an unforgettable cookie. "It has fun with your tongue," she said. "You take a bite and you get one flavor; then you chew and you get another flavor. It's not just, 'Here, have a sugar cookie.'" To those who may say that Clark's unconventional entry doesn't overtly shout "Happy Holidays," she has a response. "Sure, it's not your basic Santa cutout cookie," she said. "But it has both chocolate and cinnamon, and those are both Christmas flavors to me. Besides, to have the scent of chocolate and cinnamon in the oven, well, what's more Christmas than that?"

DOUBLE-CHOCOLATE ESPRESSO CHERRY DROPS

MAKES ABOUT 2 DOZEN COOKIES

- 1 tablespoon instant espresso powder
- 1 tablespoon boiling water
- 1 cup flour
- ¾ cup unsweetened cocoa powder
- 1 teaspoon baking soda
- ¼ teaspoon salt
- ½ cup (1 stick) unsalted butter, at room temperature

- ⅔ cup granulated sugar
- ¼ cup packed dark brown sugar
- 1 egg
- ¼ teaspoon vanilla extract
- ½ cup chopped dried cherries
- ¾ cup semisweet chocolate chips
- White chocolate for decoration, optional

Preheat the oven to 350°F and line the baking sheets with parchment paper. In a small bowl, mix the instant espresso powder and 1 tablespoon boiling water, and reserve. In a small bowl, whisk together the flour, cocoa powder, baking soda, and salt, and reserve.

In a bowl of an electric mixer on medium-high speed, beat the butter until creamy, about 1 minute. Add the granulated sugar and beat until light and fluffy, about 2 minutes. Add the dark brown sugar and beat until thoroughly combined. Add the egg and beat until thoroughly combined. Add the vanilla extract and reserved espresso mixture, and beat until thoroughly combined. Reduce the speed to low, add the flour mixture, and mix until just combined. Stir in the cherries and chocolate chips.

Using a 1-inch scoop, drop the dough 2 inches apart on the prepared baking sheets and bake for 8 to 10 minutes. Because the cookies are very dark, it's difficult to tell if they are overbaked. Watch the center of the cookies; when they lose their gooey quality, they are done. Remove the cookies from the oven and cool for 10 minutes before transferring them to a wire rack to cool completely.

If desired, in a double boiler over gently simmering water (or in a bowl in a microwave oven), melt the white chocolate and lightly drizzle over the cookies.

Faith Ford of Big Lake, Minnesota, has been faithfully making this brownie-like treat for what feels like forever. "It's a standard that I have to make, or people have a meltdown," she said with a laugh. "I bring them to work every year. People wait for them." The recipe's foundation was discovered in one of her grandmother's well-worn cookbooks, and the chocolate-with-cherry equation is rooted in another family connection. When Ford was a kid, her father would bring chocolate-covered cherries home every night between Thanksgiving and Christmas. He would give one to each of his children and then tell them if they found the box, they could eat the rest. "It wasn't until I was a teenager that I found out that he wasn't hiding them," Ford said with a laugh. "He was eating them."

FROSTED CASHEW COOKIES

MAKES ABOUT 3 DOZEN COOKIES

For cookies:

2 cups flour	1 cup firmly packed brown sugar
¾ teaspoon baking soda	1 egg
¾ teaspoon baking powder	½ teaspoon vanilla extract
¼ teaspoon salt	⅓ cup sour cream
½ cup (1 stick) unsalted butter, at room temperature	1 cup chopped salted cashews

For icing:

½ cup (1 stick) unsalted butter	¼ teaspoon vanilla extract
3 tablespoons heavy cream	2 to 2½ cups powdered sugar
	Whole salted cashews

To prepare cookies: Preheat the oven to 350°F and line the baking sheets with parchment paper. In a medium bowl, whisk together the flour, baking soda, baking powder, and salt, and reserve.

In a bowl of an electric mixer on medium-high speed, beat the butter until creamy, about 1 minute. Add the brown sugar and beat until light and fluffy, about 2 minutes. Add the egg and vanilla extract, and beat until thoroughly combined. Reduce the speed to low, and add the flour mixture in three batches, alternating with the sour cream in two batches and mixing until just combined. Fold in the chopped cashews.

Drop rounded teaspoons of the dough 2 inches apart on the prepared baking sheets and bake until the cookies are just set and turning golden around the edges, about 10 to 12 minutes. Remove the cookies from the oven and cool for 2 minutes before transferring them to a wire rack to cool completely.

To prepare icing: Melt the butter in a small saucepan over medium-high heat; then cook another 3 to 5 minutes after the butter has melted, watching carefully and swirling the pan to make sure it doesn't burn. When the butter is dark brown and smells nutty, remove from the heat. Stir in the cream and vanilla extract. Add 1½ cups powdered sugar, whisking until smooth, gradually adding more powdered sugar, 1 tablespoon at a time, until the icing is thick enough to spread. Immediately ice the cooled cookies and top each iced cookie with a whole cashew.

Two entries, one cookie: what are the odds? Both 2005 contestants share the idea that Frosted Cashew Cookies go way back. Anne Marie Draganowski of West St. Paul, Minnesota, stumbled across them while combing through her grandmother's well-worn recipe box and was instantly smitten. "You see a lot of Christmas cookies with pecans, almonds, and walnuts," she said, "but not cashews." She copied the recipe and, after just one batch, it was love at first bake. DeNae Shewmake of Burnsville, Minnesota, discovered them in an old American Crystal Sugar recipe collection, one of several hundred cookbooks lining the shelves of her constantly expanding library. The kitchen is the center of her home, and Shewmake is always expanding her cooking and baking repertoire. "I want to create new traditions for my family," she said.

Bette Revoir of St. Paul, Minnesota, bakes every week—cakes are a particular favorite—but it is the cookies she calls "sweet as a kiss" that have helped create her winning baking reputation. She's baked them for everyone, from members of the nearby police precinct and former St. Paul mayor Randy Kelly to her large (and cookie-enthusiastic) family. "When my kids were little, they would sit around the kitchen table while I was baking," she said. "I'd give them the rejects. My husband likes to lick the frosting bowl."

ORANGE KISSES
MAKES ABOUT 4 DOZEN COOKIES

Note: This dough must be prepared in advance. Be sure to buy an orange with a good rind and create a finely grated zest. You can also delve into other citrus, such as lemons.

For cookies:

- 2 **cups flour**
- ½ **teaspoon baking soda**
- ½ **teaspoon salt**
- ½ **teaspoon baking powder**
- ⅔ **cup (1 stick plus 2⅔ tablespoons) unsalted butter, at room temperature**

- ¾ **cup granulated sugar**
- 1 **egg**
- 2 **tablespoons freshly grated orange zest**
- ½ **cup freshly squeezed orange juice**

For icing:

- 2 **cups powdered sugar**
- 2 **tablespoons unsalted butter, at room temperature**

- 2 **tablespoons freshly squeezed orange juice, plus extra if needed**
- 1 **tablespoon freshly grated orange zest**

To prepare cookies: In a medium bowl, whisk together the flour, baking soda, salt, and baking powder, and reserve.

In a bowl of an electric mixer on medium-high speed, beat the butter until creamy, about 1 minute. Add the granulated sugar and beat until light and fluffy, about 2 minutes. Add the egg and beat until thoroughly combined. Add the orange zest and beat until thoroughly combined. Add the orange juice and beat for 30 seconds. Reduce the speed to low, slowly add the flour mixture, and mix until just combined. Cover the bowl with plastic wrap and refrigerate for at least 30 minutes.

When ready to bake, preheat the oven to 350°F and line the baking sheets with parchment paper. Drop rounded teaspoons of the dough 2 inches apart on the prepared baking sheets. Bake until the edges of the cookies are lightly browned, about 8 to 10 minutes. Remove the cookies from the oven and cool for 5 minutes before transferring them to a wire rack to cool completely.

To prepare icing: In a bowl of an electric mixer on low speed, mix the powdered sugar, butter, orange juice, and orange zest until combined, adding more orange juice if necessary to achieve the desired consistency. Ice cookies to taste.

PEANUT STARS SANDWICH COOKIES
MAKES ABOUT 2 DOZEN SANDWICH COOKIES

Note: This dough must be prepared in advance. Shelf-stable peanut butter, such as Jif or Skippy, works best, due to its salt and sugar content. Both raw or roasted peanuts are suitable, and both are better when toasted. To toast, place peanuts in a dry skillet over medium heat, and cook, stirring or shaking the pan frequently, until they just begin to release their fragrance, about 4 to 5 minutes (or preheat the oven to 325°F, spread nuts on an ungreased baking sheet, and bake, stirring often, for 5 to 7 minutes). Remove the nuts from the heat and cool to room temperature.

For cookies:

1¼ cups roasted, unsalted peanuts, toasted	½ cup creamy peanut butter
¾ cup flour	½ cup granulated sugar
1 teaspoon baking soda	½ cup packed light brown sugar
½ teaspoon salt	3 tablespoons whole milk
3 tablespoons unsalted butter, melted	1 egg

For filling:

¾ cup creamy peanut butter	1 cup powdered sugar
3 tablespoons unsalted butter	1 teaspoon peeled and freshly grated ginger

To prepare cookies: In a food processor, pulse the peanuts until they are finely chopped and resemble coarse crumbs (alternately, chop peanuts very fine), and reserve. In a medium bowl, whisk together the flour, baking soda, and salt, and reserve.

In a bowl of an electric mixer on medium-high speed, beat the melted butter, peanut butter, granulated sugar, and light brown sugar until smooth, about 2 minutes. Add the milk and egg, and beat until thoroughly combined. Reduce the speed to low, add the flour mixture, and mix until just combined. Fold in the peanuts. Cover the bowl with plastic wrap and refrigerate for at least 1 hour.

When ready to bake, preheat the oven to 350°F and line the baking sheets with parchment paper. Shape the dough into ½-inch balls and place 2 inches apart on the prepared baking sheets. Using moistened fingers, gently flatten cookies into 1-inch disks. Bake until the edges are slightly browned, 10 to 13 minutes. Remove the cookies from the oven and cool for 2 minutes before transferring them to a wire rack to cool completely.

To prepare filling: Place the peanut butter and butter in a small microwave-safe bowl. Cook until the mixture is easily stirred, about 30 seconds. Add the powdered sugar and ginger, and mix until filling is smooth.

To assemble cookies: Spread 1 teaspoon of the filling on the flat side of one cookie. Place the flat side of a second cookie against the filling, as if making a sandwich. Press gently, just until the filling is at edge of the cookies. Repeat with the remaining cookies.

John Halstrom and Trevor Howe of Minneapolis, Minnesota, are self-professed peanut lovers. "When I eat peanut butter—which I do, a lot—it reminds me of being a kid," said Halstrom. "My mom always made those Christmas cookies with the Hershey's Kisses." Howe fondly recalls his Massachusetts grandmother's cake-like peanut butter cookies with a peanut–ginger glaze, and Halstrom has great affection for his mother's crisp peanut butter cookies. Borrowing attributes from both, the spouses began experimenting with textures and flavors, scanning websites for guidance, until they hit recipe pay dirt. "I have a ridiculous sweet tooth," said Howe. "What I like about these cookies is that they're not overwhelmingly sweet. Your teeth don't feel like they're rotting out of your head with the first bite."

PUMPKIN COOKIES
MAKES ABOUT 3 DOZEN COOKIES

Note: Using canned pumpkin is just fine. Preferred, even.

For cookies:

3½ cups flour	½ teaspoon ground cloves
2 teaspoons baking soda	1 cup shortening
1 teaspoon salt	2 cups granulated sugar
2 teaspoons ground cinnamon	2 eggs, beaten
1½ teaspoons freshly grated nutmeg	1 cup pumpkin purée
1 teaspoon ground ginger	

For icing:

5 tablespoons brown sugar	5 tablespoons milk
3 tablespoons unsalted butter	1 cup powdered sugar, plus extra if needed

To prepare cookies: Preheat the oven to 350°F and line the baking sheets with parchment paper. In a medium bowl, whisk together the flour, baking soda, salt, cinnamon, nutmeg, ginger, and cloves, and reserve.

In a bowl of an electric mixer on medium-high speed, beat the shortening and granulated sugar until creamy, about 1 minute. Add the eggs, one at a time, beating well after each addition. Add the pumpkin purée and beat until thoroughly combined. Reduce the speed to low, add the flour mixture, and mix until just combined.

Drop rounded teaspoons of the dough 2 inches apart on the prepared baking sheets. Bake for 10 minutes; do not overbake. Remove the cookies from the oven and cool for 5 minutes before transferring them to a wire rack to cool completely.

To prepare icing: In a small saucepan over medium heat, combine the brown sugar, butter, and milk, and bring the mixture to a boil. Remove from the heat, set aside, and cool completely, about an hour. Whisk in the powdered sugar until the icing is the desired consistency, adding more if necessary. Ice cookies to taste.

For as long as she can remember, Amy Karlen of Minnetonka, Minnesota, has been crazy about the Pumpkin Cookies that her mother, Judy, makes. "For years, I've been telling Mom that this is the best cookie, that it would win contests," she said. "But I know she would never think anything she made would ever be that good." Karlen has spent a considerable amount of time turning her friends and colleagues into Pumpkin Cookie converts, too. "So many people say, 'I don't like pumpkin,' but then they like these cookies," said Karlen. "They're cakey and sweet and spicy. They have always reminded me of autumn."

The father-and-son duo of Mike and Nick Burakowski of Golden Valley, Minnesota, are serious holiday bakers, turning out twenty varieties of cookies, four cheesecakes, and a parade of Polish and German savory dishes for their annual Christmas party. "We usually spend the week before the party doing a lot of baking," said Mike. "We keep Costco very busy, buying in bulk." They discovered this recipe, an irresistible, bite-sized spin on red velvet cake, in *Southern Living* magazine.

RED VELVET WHOOPIE PIES

MAKES ABOUT 5 DOZEN SANDWICH COOKIES

Note: Keep the cookies as small as possible, about an inch in diameter. Otherwise they get to be a lot of cookie. And, yes, the recipe calls for an entire bottle of red food coloring. Be sure the mixer is going slowly when you add the food coloring.

For cookies:

- 2 **cups flour**
- 2 **tablespoons unsweetened cocoa powder**
- ½ **teaspoon baking soda**
- ¼ **teaspoon salt**
- ½ **cup (1 stick) unsalted butter, at room temperature**
- 1 **cup firmly packed brown sugar**
- 1 **egg**
- 1 **teaspoon vanilla extract**
- ½ **cup buttermilk**
- 1 **(1-ounce) bottle red food coloring**

For filling:

- 4 **tablespoons (½ stick) unsalted butter, at room temperature**
- 4 **ounces cream cheese**
- 1 **(7-ounce) jar marshmallow creme**

To prepare cookies: Preheat the oven to 375°F and line the baking sheets with parchment paper. In a large bowl, whisk together the flour, cocoa, baking soda, and salt, and reserve.

In a bowl of an electric mixer on medium-high speed, beat the butter until creamy, about 1 minute. Add the brown sugar and beat until light and fluffy, about 2 minutes. Add the egg and vanilla extract, and beat until thoroughly combined. Reduce the speed to low and add the flour mixture, in thirds, alternating with the buttermilk and beginning and ending with the flour mixture. Add the food coloring and mix well.

Drop the dough into 1-inch rounds about 1 inch apart on the prepared baking sheets. Bake until the tops are set, about 7 to 9 minutes. Remove the cookies from the oven and cool them completely on the baking sheets.

To prepare filling: In a bowl of an electric mixer on medium-high speed, beat the butter and cream cheese until smooth. Add the marshmallow creme and mix until thoroughly combined.

To assemble cookies: Spread a generous dollop of the filling on the flat side of one cookie. Place the flat side of a second cookie against the filling, as if making a sandwich. Press gently just until the filling is at the edge of the cookies. Repeat with remaining cookies. Cover and refrigerate.

RICOTTA CHEESE COOKIES
MAKES ABOUT 6 DOZEN COOKIES

Note: This makes a huge batch. You can cut the recipe in half or freeze extra cookies.

For cookies:

- 4 **cups flour**
- 2 **tablespoons baking powder**
- 1 **teaspoon salt**
- 1 **cup (2 sticks) unsalted butter, at room temperature**

- 2 **cups granulated sugar**
- 15 **ounces ricotta cheese**
- 2 **teaspoons vanilla extract**
- 2 **eggs**

For icing:

- 1½ **cups powdered sugar**
- 3 **tablespoons milk**

- **Red and green decorative sugars, optional**

To prepare cookies: Preheat the oven to 350°F and line the baking sheets with parchment paper. In a medium bowl, whisk together the flour, baking powder, and salt, and reserve.

In a bowl of an electric mixer on medium-high speed, beat the butter until creamy, about 1 minute. Add the granulated sugar and beat until light and fluffy, about 2 minutes. Reduce the speed to medium, add the ricotta cheese, vanilla extract, and eggs, and beat until thoroughly combined. Reduce the speed to low, add the flour mixture, and mix just until dough forms.

Drop tablespoons of the dough 2 inches apart on the prepared baking sheets. Bake until the cookies are lightly golden, about 15 minutes (the cookies will be soft). Remove the cookies from the oven and cool for 2 minutes before transferring them to a wire rack to cool completely.

To prepare icing: In a medium bowl, whisk together the powdered sugar and milk until smooth, adding more milk or powdered sugar as necessary for desired consistency. Using a small spatula or knife, spread the icing on the cookies (and top with decorative sugar, if desired). Allow the icing to set for 1 hour before serving.

Mary Beth Conzett of Plymouth, Minnesota, was thumbing through *Good Housekeeping* magazine when she happened upon this recipe. "I'm always looking for something different, and I love Italian food," Conzett said. "They were calling my name." It's difficult to imagine a more tender sugar cookie, and they come together in a snap. "They're so easy to make that it's almost embarrassing," she said. Turns out, it was already a winning recipe. Conzett's mother was on the lookout for a new formula for a cookie exchange and contest. "I said, 'Mom, I've got the perfect one,'" recalled Conzett, referring, of course, to Ricotta Cheese Cookies. "And she won with it."

SNOWBALL CLIPPERS

MAKES 4 TO 6 DOZEN COOKIES

Note: Use unsweetened shredded coconut for these easy-to-prepare, flavorful cookies, which taste like a Mounds bar.

½ cup flour	1 egg white, lightly beaten
¼ teaspoon baking powder	½ teaspoon vanilla extract
¾ cup granulated sugar	4 cups shredded coconut
⅓ cup sour cream	½ cup miniature chocolate chips
2 tablespoons unsalted butter, melted	4 ounces semisweet chocolate, melted

Preheat the oven to 325°F and line the baking sheets with parchment paper. In a small bowl, whisk together the flour and baking powder, and reserve.

In a bowl of an electric mixer on medium speed, beat the granulated sugar, sour cream, melted butter, and egg white until thoroughly combined. Reduce the speed to low, add the flour mixture, and mix until just combined. Add the vanilla extract and coconut, and mix until thoroughly combined. Stir in the chocolate chips.

Shape the dough into ¾-inch balls (if the dough is sticky, dampen your fingers with water), and place 1 inch apart on the prepared baking sheets. Bake just until the coconut begins to brown, about 18 to 22 minutes. Remove the cookies from the oven and cool for 2 minutes before transferring them to a wire rack to cool completely.

Line the baking sheets with wax paper. Dip the bottoms of the cooled cookies into the melted chocolate, and place the cookies, chocolate-side down, on wax paper. Refrigerate until the chocolate sets, about 30 minutes.

Becky Varone of Chaska, Minnesota, traces this recipe back to a coworker at an annual cookie exchange. For several years, a colleague supplied these coconut–chocolate cookies, and after she dropped out of the exchange, Varone asked for the recipe. "By then, I was addicted to them," Varone said with a laugh. "I still have the original recipe in her handwriting. Now I make them every year at Christmas. My family loves them."

Beth Jones of Owatonna, Minnesota, fell head-over-heels for this almond–chocolate treat when she was an exchange student in rural Sweden. A version of this cookie was the goodie her host family always had on its shopping list. On a later visit, Jones couldn't convince the store's baker to reveal the recipe. So she set out to create one for herself, gleaning elements from three Swedish-language cookbooks and several Swedish baking websites. "I wanted them to taste just like the ones I loved in Sweden," she said. "After a lot of practice, I'd say that they finally do." Jones's research discovered another reason to appreciate this hugely appealing cookie: it's flexible. "In Sweden, some are flavored with cognac or vanilla," she said. "This particular version is the one that I had when I was there, so this is the version that I like. It's all to your own taste."

SWEDISH ALMOND CHOCOLATE MACAROONS
MAKES 2 TO 3 DOZEN COOKIES

Note: This dough must be prepared in advance. Pasteurized eggs are recommended for food safety reasons. These Swedish cookies are also known as *Choklad Biskvier*.

For cookies:

- 2 (7-ounce) tubes almond paste, cut into small pieces
- 2 egg whites
- ½ cup granulated sugar

For filling:

- 1 cup (2 sticks) unsalted butter, at room temperature
- 1 cup powdered sugar
- 2 teaspoons vanilla extract
- 2 pasteurized egg yolks
- 4 teaspoons unsweetened cocoa powder

For chocolate coating:

- 10 to 12 ounces dark or bittersweet chocolate
- 2 to 4 teaspoons vegetable oil or unsalted butter, melted

To prepare cookies: In a bowl of an electric mixer on medium speed, beat the almond paste and egg whites until thoroughly combined, about 2 minutes, scraping down the sides of the bowl as necessary. Cover the bowl with plastic wrap and refrigerate for at least 30 minutes.

When ready to bake, preheat the oven to 350°F and line the baking sheets with parchment paper. Drop heaping teaspoons of the dough 2 inches apart on the prepared baking sheets. Moisten the flat bottom of a glass with water, dip into the granulated sugar, and carefully press the prepared glass bottom into a dough ball, flattening the dough; repeat with the remaining dough. Bake until lightly brown, 18 to 20 minutes. Remove the cookies from the oven and cool for 5 minutes before transferring them to a wire rack to cool completely.

To prepare filling: Line the baking sheets with wax paper. In a bowl of an electric mixer on medium speed, beat the butter until creamy, about 1 minute. Add the powdered sugar, vanilla extract, egg yolks, and cocoa powder, and mix until smooth (scraping down the sides of the bowl as necessary), about 2 minutes. Using a small knife, spread about 1 tablespoon of the filling on top of each cookie, making a rounded top. Transfer the cookies to the prepared baking sheets and refrigerate for at least 1 hour.

To prepare chocolate coating: Break the chocolate into small pieces. In a double boiler over gently simmering water (or in a bowl in a microwave oven), melt the chocolate, stirring occasionally until smooth. Whisk in 2 teaspoons of vegetable oil (or melted butter), adding more to reach the desired consistency. Let the mixture cool for a few minutes; then dip the tops of the cookies into the chocolate mixture, holding onto the almond base. Return the cookies to the prepared baking sheets and refrigerate until the chocolate hardens, at least 30 minutes. Store in the refrigerator and serve chilled.

Cutout
COOKIES

ALFAJORES
MAKES ABOUT 5 DOZEN SANDWICH COOKIES

Note: This dough must be prepared in advance. The large amount of cornstarch is correct. *Dulce de leche* (also called *cajeta* and *manjar*) is a thick caramel made from sweetened condensed milk. Find it in the international foods aisles of many supermarkets; one brand name is La Lechera. You'll find unsweetened, desiccated (dried) flaked coconut at most natural foods co-ops. This is a traditional cookie (pronounced al-fa-HOR-es) in the contestant's native Uruguay and is found all over South America.

½ cup flour, plus extra for rolling dough

1¼ cups cornstarch

1 teaspoon baking powder

½ cup (1 stick) unsalted butter, at room temperature

¾ cup granulated sugar

1 egg

1 egg yolk

Freshly grated zest of ½ lemon

1 (13.4-ounce) can dulce de leche

1½ cups coconut flakes, preferably unsweetened and desiccated

In a medium bowl, sift together the flour, cornstarch, and baking powder, and reserve. In a bowl of an electric mixer on medium-high speed, beat the butter until creamy, about 1 minute. Gradually add the granulated sugar and beat until light and fluffy, about 2 minutes. Add the egg and egg yolk, and beat until thoroughly combined. Add the lemon zest and beat until thoroughly combined. Reduce the speed to low, add the flour mixture, and mix until just combined. Cover bowl with plastic wrap and refrigerate at least 2 hours.

When ready to bake, preheat the oven to 350°F and line the baking sheets with parchment paper. On a lightly floured surface using a lightly floured rolling pin, roll the dough to ³⁄₁₆-inch thickness. Using a cookie cutter, cut the dough into rounds of desired size (between 1 and 2 inches) and place 2 inches apart on the prepared baking sheets. Repeat with the remaining dough, gathering up scraps, re-rolling, and cutting until all the dough is used. Bake 11 to 12 minutes, making sure the cookies do not brown. Remove the cookies from the oven and cool for 2 minutes before transferring them to a wire rack to cool completely. (The cookies may be stored up to a week in an airtight container before assembling.)

Spread ½ teaspoon *dulce de leche* (more for larger cookies) on the flat side of one cookie. Place the flat side of a second cookie against the *dulce de leche*, as if making a sandwich. Press gently, just until the *dulce de leche* is at the edge of the cookies. Spread a very thin layer of the *dulce de leche* onto the sandwich edge, and roll the edge in coconut flakes. Repeat with the remaining cookies.

When Graciela Cuadrado-Vielguth of Coon Rapids, Minnesota, moved north to the United States from her native Uruguay, she carried a taste of home with her: Alfajores. The delicate, buttery cookie, ubiquitous throughout South America, lacks a yuletide pedigree, but she quickly made them a staple of her Christmas baking efforts. While Alfajores require a few more steps than your basic drop cookie, they're definitely worth the extra fuss. "They're putzy," Cuadrado-Vielguth admitted. "Which is why, when my kids say, 'Why don't you make Alfajores?' I tell them, 'Okay, I'll make them, but you have to put them together.'"

ALMOND SANDWICHES

MAKES ABOUT 2 DOZEN SANDWICH COOKIES

Note: This dough must be prepared in advance. In the icing, you can substitute 1 tablespoon milk for the egg yolk. A pasteurized egg is recommended for food safety reasons.

For cookies:

1 cup (2 sticks) unsalted butter, at room temperature	1/3 cup heavy cream
	2 cups flour, plus extra for rolling dough

For icing:

4 tablespoons (1/2 stick) unsalted butter, at room temperature	1 pasteurized egg yolk
3/4 cup powdered sugar	1/2 teaspoon almond extract
	Food coloring, optional

To prepare cookies: In a bowl of an electric mixer on medium-high speed, beat the butter until creamy, about 1 minute. Add the cream and beat until thoroughly combined, occasionally scraping down the sides of the bowl. Reduce the speed to low, add the flour, and mix until just combined. Form the dough into a disk, wrap in plastic wrap, and refrigerate for at least 30 minutes.

When ready to bake, preheat the oven to 350°F and line the baking sheets with parchment paper. On a lightly floured work surface using a lightly floured rolling pin, roll the dough to 1/8-inch thickness. Using a 2-inch cookie cutter, cut the dough into desired shape (cutting out the center of half of the cookies if desired) and place 1 inch apart on the prepared baking sheets. Repeat with the remaining dough, gathering up scraps, re-rolling, and cutting until all the dough is used. Bake until the edges of the cookies are lightly browned, 15 to 20 minutes; do not overbake. Remove the cookies from the oven and cool for 2 minutes before transferring them to a wire rack to cool completely.

To prepare icing: In a bowl of an electric mixer on medium-high speed, beat the butter until creamy, about 1 minute. Reduce the speed to medium-low and add the powdered sugar, egg yolk (or milk), and almond extract, and mix until light and fluffy, about 2 minutes. Beat in the food coloring, 1 drop at a time, if desired.

To assemble cookies: Spread icing on the flat side of one cookie. Place the flat side of a second cookie (which has the extra cutout, if using) against the icing, as if making a sandwich. Press gently just until the icing is at the edge of the cookies. Repeat with the remaining cookies.

Patricia Sanford of Edina, Minnesota, has lovely stories to tell. "This recipe came down from my great-grandmother to my grandmother, to my mother, to me," she said. Although she's always called them Almond Sandwiches, other relatives refer to these family gems as plain old sugar cookies. "That would never do. They are far more than a sugar cookie," she said. "They just about melt in your mouth." Sanford is carrying the family's baking traditions forward. "My granddaughter is living with me right now, so I'm teaching her all the basics," she said. "I love that part of being a grandmother. You're not just cooking; you're telling stories. Cookies have always been a wonderful vehicle for telling stories, don't you think?"

APPLE CARDAMOM PECAN STAR COOKIES

MAKES ABOUT 1½ DOZEN SANDWICH COOKIES

Note: This dough must be prepared in advance. Commercially prepared apple butter is readily available, if you prefer not to make your own. To toast pecans, place the nuts in a dry skillet over medium heat, and cook, stirring (or shaking the pan frequently), until they just begin to release their fragrance, about 3 to 4 minutes (alternately, preheat oven to 325°F, spread the nuts on an ungreased baking sheet, and bake, stirring often, for 4 to 6 minutes). Remove the nuts from the heat and cool to room temperature. Feel free to improvise on the filling for this cookie.

For cookies:

- 2 cups flour, plus extra for rolling dough
- ½ teaspoon baking powder
- 2 tablespoons powdered sugar, plus more for decoration
- ⅛ teaspoon salt
- 2 teaspoons ground cinnamon
- 2 teaspoons ground cardamom
- ¾ cup pecans, toasted

- ½ cup (1 stick) unsalted butter, at room temperature
- ¼ cup granulated sugar
- 1 egg
- 1 teaspoon vanilla extract
- ¼ cup milk or water, as needed
- Powdered sugar, optional

For apple butter filling:

- 4 apples, peeled and sliced
- ¼ teaspoon ground cinnamon
- ¼ teaspoon ground nutmeg
- ¼ teaspoon ground cardamom

- Pinch of ground cloves
- ¼ cup brown sugar
- ½ teaspoon freshly squeezed lemon juice

To prepare cookies: In a small bowl, whisk together the flour, baking powder, powdered sugar, salt, cinnamon, and cardamom, and reserve. In a bowl of a food processor fitted with a metal blade, pulse the pecans until the nuts are very finely ground. Whisk the nuts into the flour mixture.

In a bowl of an electric mixer on medium-high speed, beat the butter until creamy, about 1 minute. Add the granulated sugar and beat until light and fluffy, about 2 minutes. Add the egg and vanilla extract, and beat until thoroughly combined. Reduce the speed to low, add the flour mixture, and mix just until combined and dough forms, adding enough milk or water to make the dough pliable. Form the dough into a disk, wrap in plastic wrap, and refrigerate until firm, at least 2 hours.

When ready to bake, preheat the oven to 375°F and line the baking sheets with parchment paper. On a lightly floured surface using a lightly floured rolling pin, roll the dough to ⅛-inch thickness. Using a star-shaped cutter (about 3 to 4 inches), cut the dough into stars. Use a smaller star-shaped cutter (about 1 to 2 inches) to cut shapes out of the center of half of the cookies (these will be the top cookies), and place 1 inch apart on the prepared baking sheets. Repeat with the remaining dough, gathering up scraps, re-rolling, and cutting until all the dough

is used. Bake until the cookies are just set and beginning to brown, about 8 to 10 minutes. Remove the cookies from the oven and cool for 2 minutes before transferring them to a wire rack to cool completely.

To prepare apple butter filling: In a saucepan over low heat, combine the apples, cinnamon, nutmeg, cardamom, cloves, brown sugar, and lemon juice, and cook until the apples are soft and can be easily mashed, about 30 to 45 minutes. Pass the mixture through a food mill (or pulse in a food processor fitted with a metal blade) to achieve a smooth consistency. There should be about ½ cup apple butter.

To assemble cookies: Spread 1 teaspoon apple butter on a bottom cookie and form a sandwich with a cutout cookie. Press gently just until the apple butter is at the edge of the cookies. Repeat with the remaining cookies. Dust with powdered sugar, if desired.

When Jana Freiband of Minneapolis, Minnesota, moved into her house, she planted a pair of what turned out to be highly productive Haralson apple trees. She channels her backyard bounty into crisps, pies, and galettes. Oh, and apple butter, which became her recipe's key ingredient. She reached for her star-shaped cookie cutter for a reason. "There's something about Christmas and stars," she said. "I've always related Christmas to something brilliant in the sky, rather than the traditional trees or wreaths. I always decorate the front of my house with stars."

CHERRY ALMOND TURNOVERS

MAKES ABOUT 4 DOZEN COOKIES

Note: This dough must be prepared in advance. Although this cookie's pie crust–meets–puff pastry dough sounds complicated, it isn't as daunting as it may appear in print. Don't be afraid to give this recipe a try—it's almost foolproof.

For filling:

- ½ **cup granulated sugar**
- 2 **tablespoons cornstarch**
- ¾ **cup minced dried tart cherries**

- ½ **cup cherry juice (preferably the more sour Montmorency type of cherry juice)**
- ½ **cup grated almond paste**

For cookies:

- 2 **cups flour, frozen, plus extra for rolling dough**
- 2 **rounded tablespoons granulated sugar**
- ¼ **teaspoon salt**
- ¾ **cup (1½ sticks) cold unsalted butter, diced**

- 2 **ounces cold cream cheese, cut into ½ -inch pieces**
- 6 to 7 **tablespoons ice water**
- 1 **egg, beaten**
- **Decorative sugar or granulated sugar**

To prepare filling: In a small saucepan over high heat, whisk together the granulated sugar and cornstarch. Whisk in the cherry juice and bring the mixture to a boil. Cook until thick, about 1 minute. Remove the pan from the heat, transfer the filling to a heatproof bowl, and cool to room temperature. Fold in the cherries and almond paste. Cover the bowl with plastic wrap and refrigerate until it is completely cold, at least 1 hour.

To prepare cookies: In a food processor fitted with a metal blade, combine the flour, granulated sugar, and salt, and pulse until combined. Add the butter and cream cheese, and pulse until the mixture resembles coarse crumbs. Add 6 to 7 tablespoons of water, 1 tablespoon at a time, and pulse until the dough starts to form marble-size clumps. Press the dough into 2 disks, wrap in plastic wrap, and refrigerate for 1 hour.

When ready to bake, preheat the oven to 400°F and line the baking sheets with parchment paper. Working with half the dough at a time, remove the dough from the refrigerator and allow to stand for 5 minutes.

On a lightly floured surface using a lightly floured rolling pin, roll the dough to 1/16-inch thickness (the dough will be quite elastic). Using a knife or a cookie cutter, cut out 2½-inch squares or circles and place them 1 inch apart on the prepared baking sheets. Repeat with the remaining dough, gathering up scraps, re-rolling, and cutting until all the dough is used.

Drop 1 teaspoon filling in the center of each square. Brush the edges of the cookies with the beaten egg, carefully fold the dough over the filling to form a triangle, and press the edges to seal (the cookies may be refrigerated at this point until ready to bake). Brush the tops of the cookies with the beaten egg and sprinkle with decorative sugar or granulated sugar.

Bake until light golden brown, 17 to 19 minutes. Remove the cookies from the oven and cool for 2 minutes before transferring them to a wire rack to cool completely.

"I love getting into the kitchen and experimenting," said Lance Swanson of North Branch, Minnesota. "It's the mad scientist in me. I'm happiest when I'm in the kitchen. Baking is kind of my meditative time." Swanson generously shares his output with friends, family, and colleagues. "They're always excited to see me when I'm carrying a tray or a plate of something," he said with a laugh. This recipe came about after walking into a bakery and spying cherry turnovers. "I thought that would make a good idea for a cookie," he said.

CHERRY PINWHEELS

MAKES ABOUT 2 DOZEN COOKIES

Note: This dough must be prepared in advance. You can prepare the dough up to two days in advance and refrigerate it until ready to use, or wrap it in plastic wrap and then aluminum foil and freeze it for up to a month. Not a fan of cherry? Almost any fruit preserve works with this festive cookie.

2½ cups flour, plus extra for rolling dough	1 cup granulated sugar
½ teaspoon salt	1 egg, separated
¾ teaspoon ground cardamom	1 teaspoon vanilla extract
1 cup (2 sticks) unsalted butter, at room temperature	⅓ cup cherry preserves
	2 tablespoons decorative sugar
4 ounces cream cheese, at room temperature	

In a medium bowl, whisk together the flour, salt, and cardamom, and reserve. In a bowl of an electric mixer on medium-high speed, beat the butter and cream cheese until creamy, about 1 minute. Add the granulated sugar and beat until light and fluffy, about 2 minutes. Add the egg yolk and vanilla extract, and beat until thoroughly combined. Reduce the speed to low and add the flour mixture in three batches, mixing just until combined and the dough forms. Divide the dough into four equal pieces, flatten each piece into a block, wrap in plastic wrap, and refrigerate until firm, at least 2 to 3 hours.

When ready to bake, preheat the oven to 350°F and line the baking sheets with parchment paper. On a lightly floured surface using a lightly floured rolling pin, roll the dough blocks (one at a time, keeping the remaining dough refrigerated until ready to roll) to ¼-inch thickness. Working quickly (the dough is easiest to work with when chilled), trim the edges to make an 8- by 12-inch rectangle. Rewrap the scraps in plastic and chill until ready to re-roll.

Using a pastry wheel, cut the rectangle into 2-inch squares. Using a spatula, transfer the squares to the prepared baking sheets, placing them 2 inches apart. With a small knife, carefully make a 1-inch-long cut in one square, from the tip of each corner in toward the center, halving each corner (you will have eight points). With the tip of the knife, lift every other point and gently fold into the center (forming a pinwheel), overlapping the ends slightly. Press the center lightly to form a small well. Brush the cookies with a lightly beaten egg white. Place ½ teaspoon of cherry preserves in the center and sprinkle with decorative sugar. Repeat this process with the remaining chilled dough and scraps.

Bake until the edges are pale and golden, 10 to 15 minutes. Remove the cookies from the oven and cool for 5 minutes before transferring them to a wire rack to cool completely.

Baking has been a lifelong avocation for Pam Hopf of Edina, Minnesota. "I started baking when I could barely reach the counter," she said. "My mother was a very good baker, and by the time I was eight years old, I was helping. When I got older, every time she'd leave the house, I'd bake something. I didn't like the supervision. Whatever I made usually turned out well, so that was my encouragement to keep going." The recipe, which Hopf encountered in *Gourmet* magazine, sounds complicated, but it is not as hard as it looks.

CLARE-OES

MAKES ABOUT 1½ DOZEN SANDWICH COOKIES

Note: This dough must be prepared in advance. Buy the best chocolate your budget permits, and don't overbake these cookies.

For cookies:

- 1¼ cups flour, plus extra for rolling dough
- 2 teaspoons instant espresso powder
- ¼ teaspoon salt
- ¾ cup (1½ sticks) unsalted butter, at room temperature
- ¾ cup granulated sugar
- 1 egg
- 1 teaspoon vanilla extract
- ¾ cup unsweetened Dutch-process cocoa powder

For buttercream filling:

- 3 tablespoons unsalted butter, at room temperature
- 1 cup plus 2 tablespoons powdered sugar
- 1 tablespoon strongly brewed coffee, plus extra if filling is too thick

To prepare cookies: In a medium bowl, whisk together the flour, espresso powder, and salt, and reserve. In a bowl of an electric mixer on medium-high speed, beat the butter until creamy, about 1 minute. Gradually add the granulated sugar and beat until light and fluffy, about 2 minutes. Add the egg and beat until thoroughly combined, scraping down the sides of the bowl as necessary. Add the vanilla extract and beat until thoroughly combined. Reduce the speed to low and gradually add the cocoa powder, scraping down the sides of the bowl as necessary and mixing until just combined. Add the flour mixture in three additions, mixing until just combined. Divide the dough into two equal pieces, shape into disks, wrap in plastic wrap, and refrigerate for at least 2 hours or overnight.

When ready to bake, preheat the oven to 325°F and line the baking sheets with parchment paper. On a lightly floured work surface using a lightly floured rolling pin, roll the dough to ¼-inch thickness. Using a 2-inch round or scalloped cookie cutter, quickly cut as many circles as possible and place 1 inch apart on the prepared baking sheets. Repeat with the remaining dough, gathering up the scraps, re-rolling, and cutting until all the dough is used.

Bake the cookies until they no longer look wet and are soft to the touch, 7 to 9 minutes; do not overbake. Remove the cookies from the oven and cool for 2 minutes before transferring them to a wire rack to cool completely.

To prepare buttercream filling: In a bowl of an electric mixer on medium-high speed, beat the butter until creamy, about 1 minute. Reduce the speed to low and gradually add the powdered sugar, scraping down the sides of the bowl as necessary. Add the coffee and mix until blended (adding more, 1 teaspoon at a time, if necessary to reach the desired consistency). Increase the speed to high and beat until the buttercream is creamy, about 2 minutes.

To assemble cookies: Spoon 1 teaspoon of the buttercream filling on the flat side of one cookie. Place the flat side of a second cookie against the filling, as if making a sandwich. Press gently just until the filling spreads evenly to about ¹⁄₁₆-inch from the edge. Repeat with the remaining cookies.

"I love all kinds of sweets, so I'm always tossing out old recipes and trying new ones," said Jane Stern of Minneapolis, Minnesota. "I have a few that I keep, but it's kind of boring to make the same old ones. I'm not exaggerating when I say that I have seventy-five dessert cookbooks." Her collection includes *The Good Cookie* by Tish Boyle, the source of this better-than-Oreos recipe. She improved on the original buttercream filling recipe by replacing Kahlua and vanilla extract with brewed coffee.

CRANBERRY-FILLED COOKIES

MAKES ABOUT 4 DOZEN COOKIES

Note: This dough must be prepared in advance.

2½ cups flour, plus extra for rolling dough	2 teaspoons vanilla extract
1 teaspoon baking powder	1 egg
¼ teaspoon salt	1½ cups dried cranberries
1 cup (2 sticks) unsalted butter, at room temperature	1 tablespoon freshly grated orange zest
1½ cups granulated sugar, divided	1½ cups water
	2 tablespoons cornstarch

In a medium bowl, sift together the flour, baking powder, and salt, and reserve. In a bowl of an electric mixer on medium-high speed, beat the butter until creamy, about 1 minute. Add 1 cup granulated sugar and beat until light and fluffy, about 2 minutes. Add the vanilla extract and beat until thoroughly combined. Add the egg and beat until thoroughly combined. Reduce the speed to low, add the flour mixture and mix until just combined. Cover the bowl with plastic wrap and refrigerate for at least 2 hours.

In a small saucepan over medium-high heat, combine the remaining ½ cup granulated sugar, cranberries, orange zest, water, and cornstarch, and cook, stirring occasionally, until thickened, about 5 minutes. Remove from heat and cool.

When ready to bake, preheat the oven to 375°F and line the baking sheets with parchment paper. On a lightly floured work surface using a lightly floured rolling pin, roll the dough to ⅛-inch thickness. Cut the dough into 3-inch circles, placing them 2 inches apart on the prepared baking sheets. Repeat with the remaining dough, gathering up the scraps, re-rolling, and cutting them until all the dough is used.

Place 1 heaping teaspoon of the cranberry mixture into the center of each cookie. Fold the edges of the dough toward the center, leaving most of the cranberry mixture uncovered. Bake until lightly browned, 12 to 15 minutes. Remove the cookies from the oven and cool for 2 minutes before transferring them to a wire rack to cool completely.

Wendy Nickel of Kiester, Minnesota, got the idea for this recipe after a visit to a cranberry festival in Warren, Wisconsin, where she was inspired by all the tempting uses she encountered for the bright red autumn berry. She went back home determined to find more ways to incorporate cranberries into her cooking. That's when she remembered the beloved raisin-filled cookie baked by her husband's grandmother. "If raisins work, why not cranberries?" she said. "I like to see what works and what doesn't. During the holidays, I love the smell of cranberries and oranges."

GRANDMA EVA'S GINGER CREAM COOKIES

MAKES ABOUT 3 DOZEN COOKIES

Note: This dough must be prepared in advance. When choosing cookie cutters for this recipe, keep it simple. The dough will stick to intricate cutters.

For cookies:

- 1 **cup (2 sticks) unsalted butter, at room temperature**
- 1 **cup granulated sugar**
- 2 **eggs**
- 1 **cup molasses**
- 2 **teaspoons ground cinnamon**
- 2 **teaspoons ground ginger**
- 1 **teaspoon baking soda**
- 1 **teaspoon cream of tartar**
- 3½ to 4 **cups flour, plus extra for rolling dough**
- 1 **cup sour cream**

For icing:

- 4 **tablespoons (½ stick) unsalted butter, at room temperature**
- 1 **teaspoon vanilla extract**
- ½ **cup milk**
- 4 **cups powdered sugar**
- **Food coloring and decorative sugars, optional**

To prepare cookies: In a bowl of an electric mixer on medium-high speed, beat the butter until creamy, about 1 minute. Add the granulated sugar and beat until light and fluffy, about 2 minutes. Add the eggs, one at a time, beating well after each addition. Add the molasses, cinnamon, ginger, baking soda, and cream of tartar, and beat until thoroughly combined. Reduce the speed to low and add the flour and sour cream in three parts, starting with flour and ending with sour cream, and mixing until just combined. If the dough is really sticky, add extra flour, 1 tablespoon at a time. Cover the bowl with plastic wrap and refrigerate overnight (or freeze for a few hours) until the dough is very stiff.

When ready to bake, preheat the oven to 350°F and line the baking sheets with parchment paper. Lightly flour a work surface and your hands. Take a handful of the dough and press it down on the work surface; then flip the dough and press again, so there is flour on both flat sides of the dough. Using a lightly floured rolling pin, roll the dough to ¼-inch thickness. Dip cookie cutters in the flour, cut the dough into desired shapes, and place 2 inches apart on the prepared baking sheets (grouping similar-size cookies on the same baking sheet to avoid burning). Repeat with the remaining dough, gathering up the scraps, re-rolling, and cutting until all the dough is used.

Bake until the cookies have puffed up a bit and a lightly pressed finger doesn't leave an indentation, about 10 minutes; do not overbake. Remove the cookies from the oven and cool for 2 minutes before transferring them to a wire rack to cool completely.

To prepare icing: In a bowl of an electric mixer on medium-high speed, beat the butter and vanilla extract until fluffy. Add the milk and beat until thoroughly combined. Reduce the speed to low and add the powdered sugar, 1 cup at a time, until the icing reaches a desired consistency. Add food coloring, if using, one drop at a time, and mix until thoroughly combined. Using a knife, spread the icing on the cookies (this recipe makes a generous amount of icing) and sprinkle with decorative sugars, if desired.

One of Patricia Bauer's happiest childhood memories is the big clear glass cookie jar in the kitchen of her grandmother's Wisconsin farm, which Eva Greismer kept stocked with giant molasses cookies glazed with sweet icing. "I remember making Ginger Creams every year for Christmas, using all of the holiday cookie cutters that we had accumulated over the years," she said. Today, Bauer, who lives in Minneapolis, Minnesota, follows a less-is-more approach. "Even though I have probably forty or fifty cookie cutters, the main one I use is the top ring from a canning jar."

KOLACHES
MAKES ABOUT 5 DOZEN COOKIES

Note: This dough must be prepared in advance. This cookie recipe is based on the Eastern European sweet yeast buns of the same name (pronounced koh-LAH-cheez). The cookies freeze beautifully.

4 **cups flour, plus extra for rolling dough**	3 **egg whites**
1 **envelope (¼ ounce) active dry yeast**	1 **cup granulated sugar**
2 **cups (4 sticks) cold unsalted butter,**	**About 2 cups apricot or raspberry**
cut into small pieces	**preserves**
2 **egg yolks**	**Powdered sugar for garnish**
1 **cup sour cream**	

In a large bowl, sift the flour. Sprinkle the yeast over the flour. Using a pastry cutter or fork, cut the butter into the flour until the mixture resembles coarse meal. Add the egg yolks and sour cream, and stir until well-combined (the dough will be thick). Cover the bowl with plastic wrap and refrigerate for at least 4 hours, preferably overnight.

When ready to bake, preheat the oven to 350°F and line the baking sheets with parchment paper. In a bowl of an electric mixer on medium-high speed, make meringue by whipping the egg whites for 2 minutes. Slowly add the granulated sugar, whipping the egg whites to stiff, glossy (but not dry) peaks, and reserve.

On a lightly floured work surface using a lightly floured rolling pin, roll 1 cup of cookie dough (keeping the remaining dough in the refrigerator so it remains firm) to the thickness of a pie crust, roughly ⅛- to ¼-inch thick. Using a 3-inch cookie cutter or a pastry or pizza cutter, cut the dough into 3-inch squares and place them 2 inches apart on the prepared baking sheets. Repeat with the remaining dough, gathering up the scraps, re-rolling, and cutting until all the dough is used.

Fill each square with ¾ teaspoon of fruit preserves and 1 generous teaspoon of meringue. Pull the corners of the cookie into the center and pinch the gathered corners together tightly. Bake the cookies until the pastry is golden brown (the cookies will reopen during baking), about 25 minutes. Remove the cookies from the oven and cool for 2 minutes before transferring them to a wire rack placed over wax paper to cool completely. To garnish, fill a wire sieve with powdered sugar and gently tap out powdered sugar over the cooled cookies.

Pat Monson Johnson of Eden Prairie, Minnesota, said that these beauties were a beloved standard in her mother's kitchen. "I'll be making these kolaches until I can't make cookies any longer," she said. "They're more like a mini-pastry, a glorified cookie. I'll go to a nice bakery and see kolaches and I'll think, 'Oh, no, they won't be as good as my cookie.'" Probably not.

LEMON–LIME CHRISTMAS TREES

MAKES ABOUT 4 DOZEN COOKIES

Note: This dough must be prepared in advance. The dough tends to be sticky, so when rolling it out, work quickly, keeping a liberal amount of flour on both the work surface and on the rolling pin.

For cookies:

3 ¾ cups flour, plus extra for rolling dough	1½ cups granulated sugar
1 teaspoon baking powder	2 eggs
1 teaspoon baking soda	2 tablespoons freshly squeezed lemon juice
¼ teaspoon salt	2 teaspoons lemon extract
1 cup (2 sticks) unsalted butter, at room temperature	1 teaspoon yellow food coloring, optional

For icing:

3 ounces cream cheese, at room temperature	½ teaspoon freshly grated lime zest
3 tablespoons unsalted butter, at room temperature	1 tablespoon freshly squeezed lime juice
	1 teaspoon green food coloring
2 cups powdered sugar	Decorative sugar, optional

To prepare cookies: In a large bowl, whisk together the flour, baking powder, baking soda, and salt, and reserve. In a bowl of an electric mixer on medium speed, beat the butter until creamy, about 1 minute. Add the granulated sugar and beat until light and fluffy, about 2 minutes. Add the eggs, one at a time, beating well after each addition. Add the lemon juice, lemon extract, and yellow food coloring (if desired), and beat until thoroughly combined. Reduce the speed to low, add the flour mixture, and mix until just combined. Form the dough into two disks, wrap in plastic wrap, and refrigerate for at least 2 hours.

When ready to bake, preheat the oven to 350°F and line the baking sheets with parchment paper. On a lightly floured surface using a lightly floured rolling pin, roll the dough to ¼-inch thickness. Using a tree cookie cutter, cut the dough and place 2 inches apart on the prepared baking sheets. Repeat with the remaining dough, gathering up scraps, re-rolling, and cutting until all the dough is used. Bake until the cookies are set but not hard, 9 to 10 minutes. Remove the cookies from the oven and cool for 2 minutes before transferring them to a wire rack to cool completely.

To prepare icing: In a bowl of an electric mixer on medium speed, beat the cream cheese and butter until creamy, about 1 minute. Reduce the speed to low, add the powdered sugar, and mix until creamy, about 2 minutes. Add the lime zest, lime juice, and food coloring, and mix until thoroughly combined. Ice cookies, and decorate with colored sugar, if desired.

Baking is a labor of love for Joan Hause of Lake Elmo, Minnesota. "I really love making cookies," she said. "I'm pretty known on both sides of our family as 'the baker.'" Hause bakes a lot of Christmas cookies each year. "I'm pretty big on the standards, but I've played with a lot of recipes to make my own version. I adapted this recipe from lemon–sugar cookies. I like the flavor of lime, so I played around with it." With Hause, appearances matter. "Christmas cookies can look good but not always taste good," she said. "I like to pay attention to both. I was happy that these cookies ended up tasting as good as they look. I entered the contest to see if other people felt the same way."

ORANGE CHOCOLATE COOKIES

MAKES ABOUT 3 DOZEN COOKIES

- 1 cup (2 sticks) unsalted butter, at room temperature, plus extra for chocolate dipping sauce
- 1 cup granulated sugar
- 1 egg yolk
- 2 teaspoons freshly grated orange zest
- 2 cups flour, plus extra for rolling dough
- ¼ cup orange marmalade, divided
- 6 ounces bittersweet chocolate

Preheat the oven to 375°F and line the baking sheets with parchment paper.

In a bowl of an electric mixer on medium-high speed, beat the butter until creamy, about 1 minute. Add the granulated sugar and beat until light and fluffy, about 2 minutes, scraping the sides of the bowl occasionally. Add the egg yolk and orange zest, and beat until thoroughly combined. Reduce the speed to low, add the flour, and mix until just combined.

On a lightly floured work surface using a lightly floured rolling pin, roll the dough to ¼-inch thickness. Using a 1½-inch round cookie cutter, cut the dough into rounds, and place 1 inch apart on the prepared baking sheets. Repeat with the remaining dough, gathering up the scraps, re-rolling, and cutting until all the dough is used. Using your thumb, make a slight indentation in the center of the cookie and fill with ¼ teaspoon orange marmalade. Bake until the edges are lightly browned, about 12 minutes. Remove the cookies from the oven and cool for 2 minutes before transferring them to a wire rack to cool completely.

In a double boiler over gently simmering water (or in a bowl in a microwave oven), melt the chocolate, whisking in enough butter (1 tablespoon at a time, up to about 4 tablespoons) to make a good dipping consistency. Dip half of each cookie in the chocolate and place on wax paper until the chocolate sets.

The heaven-made marriage of chocolate and orange has always caught the attention of Eileen Troxel of St. Paul, Minnesota. "I have loved that combination ever since I was little," she said. "It started with orange sherbet and chocolate sauce." That explains why, while thumbing through *Traditional Home* magazine a few years ago, she was immediately drawn to a butter cookie flavored with orange zest, decorated with orange marmalade, and dipped in bittersweet chocolate. The recipe quickly ascended to the top of Troxel's December baking routine. Troxel is a year-round baker, although cookies make a strictly seasonal appearance. "I leave cookies to Christmas," she said. "That makes them special."

SWEDISH SHORTBREAD COOKIES
MAKES ABOUT 3 DOZEN COOKIES

Note: This dough must be prepared in advance.

- 1 **cup (2 sticks) unsalted butter, at room temperature**
- ½ **cup plus 2 tablespoons granulated sugar**
- 2 to 2⅓ **cups flour**

- ⅓ **cup raspberry jam**
- 1 **cup powdered sugar**
- 1 **teaspoon almond extract**
- 2 to 3 **teaspoons water**

Preheat the oven to 350°F. In a bowl of an electric mixer on medium-high speed, beat the butter and granulated sugar until creamy, about 2 minutes. Reduce the speed to low and slowly add the flour, mixing until just combined, adding enough so the dough isn't sticky. Divide the dough into six balls of equal size, wrap in plastic wrap, and refrigerate for 30 minutes.

Place a dough ball between two sheets of parchment paper and, using a rolling pin, roll the dough to ¼-inch thickness, forming a 3- by 10-inch rectangle. Carefully peel away the top layer of the parchment paper.

Make a shallow crease down the center of the rectangle and fill the crease with raspberry jam. Repeat with the remaining dough. Carefully transfer the dough, retaining the parchment paper, to a baking sheet. Bake until the edges become golden brown, 10 to 12 minutes. Remove the cookies from the oven, cool for 2 minutes, and cut across the short side of the rectangle at a slight angle, making 6 or so cookies. Transfer the cookies to a wire rack to cool completely.

In a small bowl, whisk together the powdered sugar, almond extract, and 2 to 3 teaspoons of water until smooth. Using a spoon, drizzle the glaze across the cookies.

Even though the recipe didn't originate with her, Marsha Morrissette's friends and family know that Swedish Shortbread Cookies are synonymous with her and the yuletide season. "It's the only Christmas cookie I make," said the Eden Prairie, Minnesota, resident. "Everyone loves them, so why make anything else?" She first encountered the buttery treat at a cookie exchange, and it was love at first almond-and-raspberry bite. Her friend graciously shared the recipe, and a Morrissette family holiday tradition—and a contest finalist—was born. Over the years, Morrissette learned to prepare the simple beauties no earlier than a week in advance—not for freshness reasons, but because they have a tendency to disappear. "They're even good when you steal them straight out of the freezer," she said. "No defrosting necessary."

VIENNESE WAFERS WITH LEMON

MAKES ABOUT 2 DOZEN COOKIES

Note: This dough must be prepared in advance. You can substitute pecans or walnuts for the almonds if you prefer.

½ cup (1 stick) unsalted butter, at room temperature

⅓ cup granulated sugar

¼ teaspoon vanilla extract
Freshly grated zest from 1 lemon

2 teaspoons freshly chopped thyme, or 1 teaspoon dried thyme

¾ cup plus 1 tablespoon flour, plus extra for rolling dough

1 egg white, slightly beaten

¾ cup sliced almonds, roughly chopped

In a bowl of an electric mixer on medium-high speed, beat the butter until creamy, about 1 minute. Add the granulated sugar and beat until light and fluffy, about 2 minutes. Add the vanilla extract, lemon zest, and thyme, and beat until thoroughly combined. Reduce the speed to low, add the flour, and mix until just combined. Shape the dough into a disk, wrap in plastic wrap, and refrigerate for at least 1 hour or overnight.

When ready to bake, preheat the oven to 350°F and line the baking sheets with parchment paper. On a lightly floured work surface using a lightly floured rolling pin, roll the dough into a rectangular shape no less than ¼-inch thick. Trim the edges with a knife or pizza cutter and cut the dough into 1½- to 2-inch squares.

Using a pastry brush, brush the top of the wafers lightly with egg white and sprinkle with chopped almonds. Gently press the almonds into the dough. Using a thin-bladed spatula, carefully transfer the wafers to the prepared baking sheets, spacing cookies 1 inch apart. Bake until lightly browned, about 20 minutes. Remove the cookies from the oven and cool for 2 minutes before transferring them to a wire rack to cool completely.

Margaret DeHarpporte of Eden Prairie, Minnesota, has been baking this recipe for decades. "It's such a goodie that I've kept on making it," she said. "People always like them; they always ask for the recipe." Here's why: "It's basically butter and sugar, so it's nice in the mouth, so thin and crisp," she said. "It's also so simple. I like it that people can't quite put their taste buds on the thyme. It's unexpected, and I get a kick out of that." DeHarpporte is one of those bakers who is always tinkering in her kitchen. "I like to experiment," she said. "I was making muffins with lemon and thyme, and I wondered how those flavors would go with this cookie."

CUTOUT COOKIES

70

ZAZVORNIKY

MAKES ABOUT 3 DOZEN COOKIES

Note: This dough must be prepared in advance. Use a cookie cutter no wider than 2 inches—otherwise the end results are too puffy.

- 2½ cups flour, plus extra for rolling dough
- 2 teaspoons ground ginger
- 1 tablespoon baking powder
- 2 eggs

- 2 egg yolks
- 4 tablespoons (½ stick) unsalted butter, at room temperature
- 2 cups powdered sugar

Line the baking sheets with parchment paper. In a large bowl, whisk together the flour, ginger, and baking powder, and reserve. In a bowl of an electric mixer on medium-high speed, beat the eggs, egg yolks, and butter until creamy, about 2 minutes. Add the powdered sugar and beat until thoroughly combined. Reduce the speed to low, add the flour mixture, and mix until just combined.

On a lightly floured surface, with lightly floured hands, knead the dough well, adding flour if the dough is sticky. Place the dough in a large bowl, cover with plastic wrap, and refrigerate for at least 1 hour.

On a lightly floured surface using a lightly floured rolling pin, roll the dough to ½-inch thickness. Using a cookie cutter, cut the dough and place the cookies 1 inch apart on the prepared baking sheets. Repeat with the remaining dough, gathering up the scraps, re-rolling, and cutting until all the dough is used. Cover the baking sheets with plastic wrap and refrigerate overnight.

When ready to bake, preheat the oven to 350°F. Bake for 10 to 12 minutes; the cookies should double in height while baking, with the top half spongier than the bottom. Remove the cookies from the oven and cool for 2 minutes before transferring them to a wire rack to cool completely.

When Kevin Hurbanis of Minneapolis, Minnesota, was growing up, Zazvorniky were a mainstay of his Slovakian grandmother's magnet of a Christmas Eve cookie tray. The cookie with the tongue-twisting name (it's pronounced ZAHZ-vor-ni-kee) is now a cherished family tradition that the stay-at-home dad shares with his two children, Jack and Emma. For as long as he can remember, Hurbanis has been making the soft, ginger-cast cookie using the same notched rectangular cookie cutter, although most any cookie cutter will do. Along with the recipe, that special cutter is a treasured memento from his grandmother's kitchen. "It's a nice connection that I have to her," he said, "and an especially nice one that I can share with my kids."

Refrigerator COOKIES

ALMOND PALMIERS
MAKES 2 TO 3 DOZEN COOKIES

Note: This dough must be prepared in advance. Palmiers (pronounced pahlm-YAYs) go by many other names, including elephant ears, palm leaves, and French hearts. Widely available Pepperidge Farm puff pastry works perfectly well with this cookie, but we loved the results we got using Dufour Pastry Kitchens puff pastry, which is more expensive. It's worth seeking out, because the all-butter product makes a gloriously light, golden, and flaky palmier.

4 tablespoons (½ stick) unsalted butter, at room temperature	1 egg
¼ cup powdered sugar, plus extra for garnish, optional	½ teaspoon almond extract
1 (7-ounce) tube almond paste, cut into small pieces	¼ cup granulated sugar, divided
	1 (17.3-ounce) package puff pastry sheets (containing 2 sheets), refrigerated

In a bowl of an electric mixer on medium-high speed, beat the butter until creamy, about 1 minute. Add the powdered sugar and almond paste. Beat until creamy, about 1 minute. Add the egg and almond extract, and beat until thoroughly combined.

Sprinkle a surface with 1 tablespoon granulated sugar. Carefully unfold 1 puff pastry sheet over the granulated sugar and sprinkle with 1 tablespoon granulated sugar. Using a rolling pin, roll the puff pastry sheet into a 12-inch square. Divide the almond paste mixture in half, and carefully spread half the mixture evenly over the top of the puff pastry sheet. Carefully roll up opposite sides of the puff pastry sheet, from the outer edge to the middle, with the rolls meeting in the center. Firmly press together, wrap the dough logs in plastic wrap, and refrigerate for at least 2 hours and up to 2 days. Repeat with the second puff pastry sheet.

When ready to bake, preheat the oven to 400°F and line the baking sheets with parchment paper. Unwrap the puff pastry logs and, using a sharp knife, trim off the uneven ends. Cut the dough into ¼-inch slices and place (flat side down) 2 inches apart on the prepared baking sheets. Bake until golden brown, 12 to 14 minutes. Remove the cookies from the oven and cool for 2 minutes before transferring them to a wire rack to cool completely. Dust with powdered sugar, if desired, and serve.

A last-minute need to fill out a holiday cookie tray found Kay Lieberherr of St. Paul, Minnesota, turning to the palmiers at Surdyk's in Minneapolis. "It turned out that everyone asked for the recipe for the palmiers, and not for the cookies that I had baked," she said with a laugh. That response sent her on a mission to develop her own palmier recipe. Using commercially prepared puff pastry makes this recipe a snap to prepare. "I love it when you don't spend a lot of time on something, yet people think, 'Wow, that must have taken days,'" said Lieberherr.

CAPPUCCINO FLATS
MAKES ABOUT 4 DOZEN COOKIES

Note: This dough must be prepared in advance. We prefer using instant espresso coffee (such as the Medaglia d'Oro brand, available at most supermarkets) instead of instant coffee crystals. To prepare a gluten-free version, substitute with a ratio of ¾ cup gluten-free flour for 1 cup all-purpose flour.

For cookies:

2 cups flour	1 cup (2 sticks) unsalted butter, at room temperature
1 teaspoon ground cinnamon	
¼ teaspoon salt	½ cup granulated sugar
2 ounces unsweetened chocolate	½ cup brown sugar, packed
1 tablespoon instant coffee crystals	1 egg
1 teaspoon water	

For icing:

1½ cups semisweet chocolate pieces	3 tablespoons shortening

To prepare cookies: In a large bowl, whisk together the flour, cinnamon, and salt, and reserve. In a double boiler over gently simmering water (or in a bowl in a microwave oven), melt the unsweetened chocolate, stirring occasionally until smooth. Remove from the heat and cool slightly.

In a small bowl, combine the coffee crystals and 1 teaspoon water, and stir until dissolved. In a bowl of an electric mixer on medium-high speed, beat the butter until creamy, about 1 minute. Add the granulated sugar and brown sugar, and beat until light and fluffy, about 2 minutes. Add the melted chocolate, coffee mixture, and egg, and beat until thoroughly combined. Reduce the speed to low, add the flour mixture, and mix until just combined. Cover the bowl with plastic wrap and refrigerate for at least 1 hour.

When the dough is easy to handle, divide in half and shape into logs of about 7 inches in length and 1 inch in diameter. Wrap the dough logs in plastic wrap and refrigerate for at least 6 hours or overnight.

When ready to bake, preheat the oven to 350°F and line the baking sheets with parchment paper. Unwrap the dough and, using a sharp knife, trim off the uneven ends. Cut the dough into ¼-inch slices and place 1 inch apart on the prepared baking sheets. Bake until the edges are firm and lightly browned, about 10 to 12 minutes. Remove the cookies from the oven and cool for 2 minutes before transferring them to a wire rack to cool completely.

To prepare icing: In a double boiler over gently simmering water (or in a bowl in a microwave oven), melt the semisweet chocolate and shortening, whisking to combine. Remove the chocolate from the heat and let the mixture cool for a few minutes. Dip one half of each cookie into the chocolate mixture, sliding the back of the cookie on the edge of the pan to remove excess chocolate. Place the cookies on wax paper until the chocolate sets.

Dianne Sivald of White Bear Lake, Minnesota, says cookies are her favorite part of Christmas. She discovered Cappuccino Flats in a *Better Homes and Gardens* cookbook "so long ago that I can't remember the exact date," she said. It wouldn't be Christmas at the Sivald home without these elegant, richly flavored cookies, which she adapted from the original recipe. "They're so good that I sometimes wonder why I make them only at Christmas," she said. "But maybe that's what makes them so special. You have to wait for them."

CINNAMON BUN COOKIES
MAKES 3 TO 4 DOZEN COOKIES

Note: This dough must be prepared in advance. Because cinnamon is the recipe's centerpiece ingredient, it may well be worth splurging on a top-notch cinnamon, such as Vietnamese Extra Fancy ground cinnamon at Penzeys (penzeys.com). You can also minimize holiday baking stress by preparing this dough in advance and freezing it.

For cookies:

3 cups flour

1 teaspoon baking powder

1 teaspoon baking soda

½ teaspoon salt

½ cup (1 stick) unsalted butter, at room temperature

2 tablespoons (1 ounce) cream cheese, at room temperature

1 cup powdered sugar

1 egg

2 teaspoons vanilla extract

For filling:

6 tablespoons (¾ stick) unsalted butter, at room temperature

¾ cup dark brown sugar, packed

1 tablespoon ground cinnamon

⅛ teaspoon salt

For icing:

6 tablespoons (¾ stick) unsalted butter, at room temperature

¼ cup (2 ounces) cream cheese, at room temperature

Pinch of salt

½ teaspoon vanilla extract

¼ teaspoon almond extract

2 cups powdered sugar

To prepare cookies: In a large bowl, whisk together the flour, baking powder, baking soda, and salt, and reserve. In a bowl of an electric mixer on medium-high speed, beat the butter and cream cheese until creamy, about 1 minute. Reduce the speed to low, add the powdered sugar, and mix until light and fluffy, about 2 minutes. Add the egg and vanilla extract, and mix until thoroughly combined. Gradually add the flour mixture, mixing just until a smooth dough is formed. Divide the dough into two equal pieces and flatten into disks. Wrap the dough in plastic wrap and refrigerate while preparing the filling.

To prepare filling: In a bowl of an electric mixer on medium speed, beat the butter, brown sugar, cinnamon, and salt until smooth. Remove one dough disk and place between two large pieces of parchment or wax paper. Roll the dough to a 9- by 12-inch rectangle (lifting the top piece of the paper and piecing/re-rolling the dough as necessary); then remove the top paper. Dot teaspoon-size pieces of the filling over half of the dough (using half of the filling), and use the back of a spoon to evenly spread the filling across the top of the dough.

Beginning with one long edge, gently roll up the dough, peeling away the bottom layer of parchment or wax paper and taking care not to allow cracks in the dough to appear. Place the

dough seam-side down (and gently stretch from the center outward to form a 12-inch long roll, if necessary). Using a sharp knife, cut the roll in half. Wrap the dough logs in plastic wrap and refrigerate for at least 2 hours or overnight (or the dough may be covered well and frozen; thaw it in the refrigerator before baking). Repeat with the remaining dough disk and filling.

When ready to bake, preheat the oven to 375°F and line the baking sheets with parchment paper. Unwrap the dough logs and, using a sharp knife, trim off the uneven ends. Cut the dough into ¼-inch slices and place the cookies 2 inches apart on the prepared baking sheets. Bake until the cookies are just set and the edges barely begin to brown, about 8 to 9 minutes. Remove the cookies from the oven and cool for 2 minutes before transferring them to a wire rack to cool completely.

To prepare icing: While the cookies are in the oven, combine the butter, cream cheese, salt, almond extract, and vanilla extract in the bowl of an electric mixer on medium-high speed. Beat until creamy, about 1 minute. Reduce the speed to low, add the powdered sugar, and mix until smooth.

When the cookies are still warm, top each cookie with about 1½ teaspoons icing, and gently spread the icing on the cookies (or fill a pastry bag fitted with a small tip and pipe the icing over the cookies). Cool the cookies completely; then refrigerate until the icing sets. Store the cookies in a tightly covered container in the refrigerator, and serve at room temperature.

Patrice Hurd of Bemidji, Minnesota, created a cookie that looks and tastes like a cinnamon bun, one that blossomed out of her Finnish grandmother's reputation as "queen of the cinnamon bun." "You walked into her house and the countertops and table were covered with them," Hurd said. "She baked. She shared. It was a communal experience."

CRANBERRY PECAN SWIRLS

MAKES ABOUT 3 DOZEN COOKIES

Note: This dough must be prepared in advance.

1½ **cups flour, plus extra for rolling dough**	1 **egg**
¼ **teaspoon baking powder**	1 **teaspoon vanilla extract**
¼ **teaspoon salt**	⅓ **cup finely chopped fresh cranberries**
½ **cup (1 stick) unsalted butter, at room temperature**	½ **cup ground pecans**
¾ **cup granulated sugar**	1 **tablespoon freshly grated orange zest**

In a medium bowl, whisk together the flour, baking powder, and salt, and reserve. In a bowl of an electric mixer on medium-high speed, beat the butter and granulated sugar until light and fluffy, about 2 minutes. Add the egg and vanilla extract, and beat until thoroughly combined. Reduce the speed to low, add the flour mixture, and mix until just combined. Cover the bowl with plastic wrap and refrigerate for at least 1 hour.

In a small bowl, combine the cranberries, pecans, and orange zest. On a lightly floured surface using a lightly floured rolling pin, roll the dough to a 10-inch square. Sprinkle the cranberry mixture over the dough, leaving a ½-inch border on two opposite sides. Roll the dough, jelly-roll fashion, beginning at one of the borders and rolling toward the other border. Wrap the dough log in plastic wrap and freeze for at least 8 hours.

When ready to bake, preheat the oven to 375°F and line the baking sheets with parchment paper. Unwrap the dough log and, using a sharp knife, trim off the uneven ends. Cut the dough into ¼-inch thick slices and place 2 inches apart on the prepared baking sheets. Bake until lightly browned, 14 to 15 minutes. Remove the cookies from the oven and cool for 2 minutes before transferring them to a wire rack to cool completely.

"We're okay with chocolate, but our family thing is cranberries—we love them," said Annette Poole of Prior Lake, Minnesota, who proceeded to detail an impressive list of favorite sauces, pies, and cakes that put the scarlet berry in the spotlight. "I could be their spokesperson." While on a vacation, Poole stumbled across this recipe in a book, and it grabbed her eye. "I like the pictures; that's what sells it for me," she said. "If I see something that appeals to me visually, then I'll make it." She made a copy and set it aside. Fast-forward a few years. She finally baked it, and flipped over it. "One of the reasons I like it is because it's not too sweet; there's not a lot of sugar in the filling," she said. "And yes, the fresh cranberries. I'm always on the lookout for anything cranberry. If there's a cranberry recipe, I've got to have it."

KOROVA COOKIES
MAKES ABOUT 3 DOZEN COOKIES

Note: This dough must be prepared in advance. Sea salt (the surprise ingredient in this "grown-up cookie") puts an unexpectedly glamorous gloss on humble slice-and-bake refrigerated cookies. That little bit of crunchy French sea salt makes the cookie feel not quite so sweet. This recipe calls specifically for sel de guérande, a gray sea salt that is harvested from the salt marshes of Brittany and is available at many specialty cooking stores, but feel free to substitute other sea salts.

- 1¼ cups flour
- ⅓ cup unsweetened cocoa powder
- ½ teaspoon sel de guérande or other coarse sea salt
- ½ teaspoon baking soda
- ½ cup plus 3 tablespoons (1 stick plus 3 tablespoons) unsalted butter, at room temperature
- ⅔ cup firmly packed brown sugar
- ¼ cup granulated sugar
- 1 teaspoon vanilla extract
- 5 ounces (about ¾ cup) semisweet chocolate chips

In a medium bowl, whisk together the flour, cocoa powder, sea salt, and baking soda, and reserve. In a bowl of an electric mixer on medium-high speed, beat the butter until creamy, about 1 minute. Add the brown sugar, granulated sugar, and vanilla extract, and beat until light and fluffy, about 2 minutes. Reduce the speed to low, add the flour mixture, and mix until crumbly, just enough so flour is not blowing all over the bowl. Fold in the chocolate chips.

On a clean surface, knead the dough a few times to finish mixing (the warmth of your hands will help the mixture come together). Divide the dough in half and shape into logs about 18 inches in length and about 1 inch in diameter. Wrap the dough logs in plastic wrap and refrigerate for at least 1 hour or for up to 3 days.

When ready to bake, preheat the oven to 325°F and line the baking sheets with parchment paper. Unwrap the dough logs and, using a sharp knife, trim off the uneven ends. Cut the dough into ½-inch slices (if the cookies come apart after slicing, just push the dough back together using your fingers) and place 1 inch apart on the prepared baking sheets. Bake 12 minutes; do not overbake. Remove the cookies from the oven and cool 5 minutes before transferring them to a wire rack to cool completely.

Always on the lookout for anything chocolate, Mary Eckmeier of St. Paul, Minnesota, plucked this recipe from *Paris Sweets* by Dorie Greenspan and then, as is her custom, stamped it with her own imprint. "The author said to cut up chocolate, but chips are so much easier," she said. While the original recipe calls for coarse sea salt, Eckmeier gets a little more specific and uses sel de guérande, harvested from the salt marshes of Brittany.

NANCY'S ANISE–PECAN COOKIES

MAKES ABOUT 4 DOZEN COOKIES

Note: This dough must be prepared in advance.

2½ cups flour

1 teaspoon baking soda

½ teaspoon salt

½ teaspoon ground cloves

½ teaspoon ground cinnamon

1 tablespoon anise seeds

1 cup (2 sticks) unsalted butter, at room temperature

1 cup granulated sugar

1 cup firmly packed brown sugar

2 eggs

½ cup finely chopped pecans

In a large bowl, whisk together the flour, baking soda, salt, cloves, cinnamon, and anise seeds, and reserve. In a bowl of an electric mixer on medium-high speed, beat the butter, granulated sugar, and brown sugar until light and fluffy, about 2 minutes. Add the eggs, one at a time, beating well after each addition. Reduce the speed to low and add the flour mixture in thirds, mixing until combined. Stir in the pecans. Divide the dough in half and shape the dough into two logs, each 10 inches long. Wrap the dough logs in wax paper and refrigerate for at least 4 hours or overnight.

When ready to bake, preheat the oven to 350°F and line the baking sheets with parchment paper. Unwrap the dough logs and, using a sharp knife, trim off the uneven ends. Cut the dough into ¼-inch slices and place 2 inches apart on the prepared baking sheets. Bake for 9 to 10 minutes. Remove the cookies from the oven and cool for 2 minutes before transferring them to a wire rack to cool completely.

Mary Jane Nickerson of Montevideo, Minnesota, is a cookie fan. "They're not like a piece of cake, you know?" she said. "You can have a little cookie, or two of them, and not feel guilty." She came by this recipe through the help of a friend. "My friend Nancy Harrington lives in New Bedford, Massachusetts, and when we lived near there, I used to get cookies every Christmas from her," she said. "These were the best ones. I used to rummage through the tin every year and eat them first. When I had to move, I asked her, 'Would you be willing to part with the recipe?' Nancy thinks it might be an old Pillsbury recipe from the 1940s or 1950s that she altered. She's always taking liberties with recipes, making them better." Anise is the attention-grabber. "It's a different flavor from your regular Christmas cookies," she said. "It's a surprise, you know?"

"I love pistachios," said Linda McEwen of Mahtomedi, Minnesota. "For whatever the reason, they've really become popular over the past couple of years. I suppose they're healthier than peanuts. I think it's fun that they're green. It fits in with Christmas." McEwen originally found this recipe in *Midwest Living* magazine.

PISTACHIO PINE CONES

MAKES ABOUT 4 DOZEN COOKIES

Note: This dough must be prepared in advance. If salted, dry-roasted pistachios are unavailable, toast and salt them yourself. Place nuts in a dry skillet over medium heat, sprinkle with ½ teaspoon salt, and cook, stirring or shaking the pan frequently, until they just begin to release their fragrance, about 2 to 3 minutes (or preheat oven to 325°F, spread nuts on an ungreased baking sheet, sprinkle with ½ teaspoon salt, and bake, stirring often, for 4 to 6 minutes). Remove the nuts from the heat and cool to room temperature. Chop all the nuts before beginning the recipe. This recipe also works well with gluten-free flour mix, such as the Cup4Cup brand, and with semisweet or bittersweet chocolate.

1 **cup (2 sticks) unsalted butter, at room temperature**	2 **cups flour**
¾ **cup granulated sugar**	2 **cups finely chopped salted, dry-roasted pistachios, divided**
½ **teaspoon vanilla extract**	12 **ounces white chocolate**
¼ **teaspoon salt**	1 **tablespoon vegetable shortening**
1 **vanilla bean**	

In a bowl of an electric mixer on medium-high speed, beat the butter for 30 seconds. Add the granulated sugar, vanilla extract, and salt, and beat until just combined, scraping down the sides of the bowl occasionally. Split the vanilla bean in half lengthwise. Using the tip of a paring knife, scrape the seeds from the bean into the butter mixture, and beat until thoroughly combined. Reduce the speed to low, add the flour in ½-cup increments, and mix just until combined. Stir in 1 cup of the pistachios.

Divide the dough in half and shape each half into logs measuring 1½-inches in diameter, giving the log an oval shape (one with distinctive wider and narrower ends) so that the cut cookies will resemble a pine-cone shape. Wrap the dough logs in plastic wrap and refrigerate for at least 2 hours or up to 2 days.

When ready to bake, preheat the oven to 375°F and line the baking sheets with parchment paper. Unwrap the dough logs and, using a sharp knife, trim off the uneven ends. Cut the dough into ¼-inch slices and place 1 inch apart on the prepared baking sheets. Bake until just firm and browned on the bottoms, about 10 to 12 minutes. Remove the cookies from the oven and cool for 2 minutes before transferring them to a wire rack to cool completely.

In a double boiler over gently simmering water (or in a bowl in a microwave oven), melt the white chocolate and shortening, stirring to combine. Place the remaining 1 cup of chopped pistachios in a wide bowl. Dip the wider end of each cookie in the melted white chocolate (to resemble a pine cone), then dip in the pistachios. Transfer the cookies to wax paper and let stand until set.

TART AND SASSY CRANBERRY LEMON DROPS

MAKES ABOUT 3 DOZEN COOKIES

Note: This dough must be prepared in advance. To toast pecans, place the nuts in a dry skillet over medium heat, and cook, stirring or shaking the pan frequently, until they just begin to release their fragrance, about 3 to 4 minutes (alternately, preheat oven to 325°F, spread the nuts on an ungreased baking sheet, and bake, stirring often, for 4 to 6 minutes). Remove the nuts from the heat and cool to room temperature.

For cookies:

- ¾ cup granulated sugar
  Zest from 2 large lemons
- ½ cup dried cranberries
- ½ cup toasted pecans
- 1¾ cups flour
- ¼ teaspoon salt
- ¼ teaspoon baking powder
- ¾ cup (1½ sticks) very cold unsalted butter, cut into ½-inch cubes
- 2 tablespoons freshly squeezed lemon juice
- 1 egg yolk
- ½ teaspoon vanilla extract

For icing:

- 1 tablespoon cream cheese, at room temperature
- 1 tablespoon unsalted butter, at room temperature
- 1 to 2 tablespoons freshly squeezed lemon juice
- 1½ cups powdered sugar
- ¼ teaspoon vanilla extract
  Zest from 1 large lemon
  Dried cranberries
- 15 lemon drop candies, crushed

To prepare cookies: In a food processor fitted with a metal blade, combine the granulated sugar, lemon zest, and dried cranberries, and process until thoroughly combined, about 30 to 45 seconds. Add the pecans and process an additional 15 seconds.

In a medium bowl, whisk together the flour, salt, and baking powder. Add the flour mixture to the sugar mixture and combine with ten 1-second pulses. Scatter the cold butter pieces on top of the sugar-flour mixture and pulse for fifteen 1-second pulses.

In a small bowl, whisk together the egg yolk, lemon juice, and vanilla extract. With the food processor running, add the egg mixture in a slow, steady stream, until the dough begins to form into a ball, about 10 to 15 seconds.

Remove the dough from the food processor and divide it in half. Place the balls of dough between sheets of parchment paper and roll the dough into logs 1½-inches in diameter. Wrap the dough logs in plastic wrap and refrigerate for at least 2 hours.

When ready to bake, preheat the oven to 375°F and line the baking sheets with parchment paper. Unwrap the dough logs and, using a sharp knife, trim off the uneven ends. Cut the dough into ⅜-inch slices and place 1 inch apart on prepared baking sheets. Bake until the centers of the cookies begin to color and the edges are a light golden brown, about 13 to 16 minutes. Remove the cookies from the oven and cool for 2 minutes before transferring them to a wire rack to cool completely.

To prepare icing: In a bowl of an electric mixer on medium speed, combine the cream cheese, butter, lemon juice, powdered sugar, vanilla extract, and lemon zest, and mix until smooth. Transfer the icing to a piping bag fitted with a small tip. Squeeze a drop of icing (about the size of a quarter) onto the center of the cookie, top with 2 to 3 dried cranberries, and sprinkle the tops of the cookies with crushed lemon drops.

The recipe is a cross between two different cookies that Janet Heirigs of Minneapolis, Minnesota, has been baking for years. The base is a glazed lemon cookie from *Cook's Illustrated* magazine, and the embellishments were inspired by a Martha Stewart biscotti, one that puts cranberries and pecans front and center. Heirigs often enlists her colleagues in the taste-testing process. This time around, she also turned to a group of nuns at a Franciscan retreat she attends several times a year in Annandale, Minnesota. Turns out they weren't impressed with a time-consuming cranberry flourish, and Heirigs dropped it. "Then again, they have a 'living simply' belief," she said with a laugh. Still, our judges remained impressed. "So pretty," said one. "This is what a holiday cookie looks like," added another.

Rolled
COOKIES

ACORN COOKIES

MAKES ABOUT 3 DOZEN COOKIES

For cookies:

1 cup (2 sticks) unsalted butter	⅓ cup finely chopped pecans
¾ cup firmly packed dark brown sugar	2½ cups flour
1 teaspoon vanilla extract	½ teaspoon baking powder

For topping:

24 caramels, unwrapped	¾ cup chopped pecans
⅛ to ¼ cup water	

To prepare cookies: Preheat the oven to 350°F and line the baking sheets with parchment paper. In a medium saucepan over low heat, melt the butter. Remove the pan from the heat, transfer the butter to a large bowl, and stir in the brown sugar, vanilla extract, and pecans.

In a medium bowl, whisk together the flour and baking powder. Add the flour mixture to the butter mixture and mix until thoroughly combined.

Shape the dough into 1-inch balls and place 2 inches apart on the prepared baking sheets. Flatten the balls on the bottoms and pinch the tops to form a point so the dough resembles an acorn. Bake until golden brown, 15 to 18 minutes. Remove the cookies from the oven and cool for 2 minutes before transferring them to a wire rack to cool completely.

To prepare topping: In a double boiler over gently simmering water (or in a bowl in a microwave oven), melt the caramels. Add ⅛ cup water to thin the melted caramel, adding more water, 1 teaspoon at a time, until the caramel sauce reaches spreading consistency. Dip the flat side of each cookie into the caramel sauce and then into chopped pecans. Transfer the cookies to wax paper until the caramel sets.

ROLLED COOKIES

94

When Barbara Melom of Minneapolis, Minnesota, moved to Minnesota from Pennsylvania in the late 1960s, she was taken with the cookie traditions she found in her new home state: krumkake, sandbakkels, and other delicate delicacies. "In Pennsylvania we baked sturdy cookies," she said. "Lots of raisins and nuts, really dense and heavy." When the calendar rolls around to Christmas baking, Melom adheres to one rule: no rolling pins. This is one reason why the retired speech therapist has been making Acorn Cookies for thirty-five years: they look complicated, but they're just two easy steps beyond a simple drop cookie. They're one of eight to ten varieties that Melom bakes each December, when she showers her friends and acquaintances with cookies. "If you ask me, a cup of coffee and a good cookie is one of life's simple pleasures," she said.

BACON CORNMEAL VENETOS

MAKES 3 TO 4 DOZEN COOKIES

Note: Imitation maple flavoring is used in the frosting to bump up its flavor. For the cookies, use the real thing.

For cookies:

¾ cup golden raisins	6 tablespoons pure maple syrup
1 cup finely ground yellow cornmeal	(Grade B preferred)
1½ cups flour	2 eggs
1½ teaspoons baking powder	1 teaspoon vanilla extract
Pinch of salt	4 bacon strips, cooked and chopped into
1 cup (2 sticks) unsalted butter,	small pieces, about ½ cup
at room temperature	

For glaze:

1 tablespoon unsalted butter	¼ teaspoon imitation maple flavoring
1 cup powdered sugar	2 tablespoons milk

To prepare cookies: Preheat the oven to 350°F and line the baking sheets with parchment paper. In a small bowl, cover the raisins with warm water and soak for 15 minutes. Strain, reserving the raisins. In a medium bowl, whisk together the cornmeal, flour, baking powder, and salt, and reserve.

In a bowl of an electric mixer on medium-high speed, cream the butter and maple syrup until light and fluffy, about 2 minutes. Add the eggs, one at a time, beating well after each addition. Add the vanilla extract and beat until thoroughly combined. Reduce the speed to low, add the flour mixture, and mix until just combined. Stir in the raisins and bacon.

Shape the dough into 1-inch balls. Place the balls 2 inches apart on the prepared baking sheets. Bake until golden brown on the edges, about 10 minutes. Remove the cookies from the oven and cool for 2 minutes before transferring them to a wire rack to cool completely.

To prepare glaze: In a saucepan over medium heat, melt the butter and cook until butter turns brown; do not burn. Remove the pan from the heat. Add the powdered sugar, maple flavoring, and milk, and whisk until the glaze is smooth and a single consistent color. Drizzle the glaze on the cooled cookies.

This group of high school friends from Minnesota—Julie Bollmann of Chanhassen, Wendy Kleiser of Minneapolis, Joan Koller of Jordan, Geri Olson of Shoreview, and Mary Urbas of Woodbury—gathers for an annual early December cookie bake and exchange. "We call ourselves the Cookie Chicks," said Bollmann, noting that the club also includes matching aprons and annual recipe scrapbooks. "Now we also have a couple of daughters who are participating—we call them the Chicklets." Bollmann always test-drives a few recipes from the *Star Tribune*'s Taste Holiday Cookie Contest, and she proposed that they submit a recipe to the competition. The rest is history. Bollmann assures first-timers that this drop-cookie formula is an easy one. "Let's put it this way," she said with a laugh, "if I can make it, anyone can make it. Besides, bacon in a cookie is a good excuse to have cookies for breakfast."

BRANDY CHERRY COOKIES
MAKES ABOUT 3 DOZEN COOKIES

Note: This dough must be prepared in advance. Five-spice powder is a blend of equal parts cinnamon, cloves, fennel seed, star anise, and Szechuan peppercorns. You can find it in the spice aisles of most supermarkets. If the cherries are large, chop them. Don't overwork this dough, or you may end up with flattened cookies. Refrigerating the dough can help the cookies hold their shape. Feel free to experiment with different varieties of fruit brandy.

- 1 **cup dried cherries**
- ½ **cup brandy**
- 2½ **cups flour, plus extra if needed**
- ¼ **teaspoon salt**
- ½ **teaspoon five-spice powder**

- 1 **cup (2 sticks) unsalted butter, at room temperature**
- 1 **cup granulated sugar, divided**
- 1 **egg**
- 1 **egg yolk**

In a small saucepan over medium heat, combine the dried cherries and brandy. When the brandy starts to simmer, remove the pan from the heat and let stand for 30 minutes. Drain, reserving both the cherries and the liquid.

In a medium bowl, whisk together the flour, salt, and five-spice powder, and reserve. In a bowl of an electric mixer on medium-high speed, beat the butter until light and fluffy, about 2 minutes. Add ¾ cup granulated sugar and beat until thoroughly combined, about 1 minute. Add the egg, egg yolk, and 2 teaspoons of the reserved brandy liquid (discard the remaining liquid), and beat until thoroughly combined. Reduce the speed to low and add the flour mixture, mixing just until combined. Do not overmix (if the dough is sticky, add more flour, 1 tablespoon at a time; you need to be able to roll the dough into balls in your hands). Stir in the drained cherries. Shape the dough into 1-inch balls and refrigerate for at least 2 hours or overnight.

When ready to bake, preheat the oven to 350°F and line the baking sheets with parchment paper. Place the remaining ¼ cup granulated sugar in a shallow bowl. Roll the dough balls in the sugar to coat; then place 1 inch apart on the prepared baking sheets. Bake until lightly browned and set on the edges, about 10 to 12 minutes. Remove the cookies from the oven and cool for 2 minutes before transferring them to a wire rack to cool completely.

Kathleen Sonsteng of Laporte, Minnesota, found this recipe in *Country Home* magazine, and she reserves it for December. "A few years ago, I gave the recipe to a friend, and they make them year-round," she said. "But I keep it special and only make them on the holidays. As soon as I made this recipe for the first time, in 2008, it became a Christmas standard. It has become a tradition in our house, and I give it to others, because everyone loves it."

CARDAMOM COOKIES

MAKES ABOUT 2 DOZEN COOKIES

For cookies:

½ teaspoon baking soda

1 teaspoon ground cardamom

1 teaspoon ground cinnamon

1½ cups flour

½ cup (1 stick) unsalted butter, at room temperature

1 cup granulated sugar

1 egg

For icing:

4 tablespoons (½ stick) unsalted butter, at room temperature

1 teaspoon vanilla extract

½ cup milk

½ teaspoon ground cardamom

½ teaspoon ground cinnamon

4 cups powdered sugar

To prepare cookies: Preheat the oven to 350°F and line the baking sheets with parchment paper. In a small bowl, whisk together the baking soda, cardamom, cinnamon, and flour, and reserve.

In a bowl of an electric mixer on medium-high speed, beat the butter until creamy, about 1 minute. Add the granulated sugar and beat until light and fluffy, about 2 minutes. Add the egg and beat until thoroughly combined. Reduce the speed to low, add the flour mixture, and mix until just combined.

Shape the dough into balls and place 2 inches apart on the prepared baking sheets. Carefully press the dough with the flat bottom of a glass and bake until lightly browned, 14 to 16 minutes. Remove the cookies from the oven and cool for 2 minutes before transferring them to a wire rack to cool completely.

To prepare icing: In a bowl of an electric mixer on medium-high speed, beat the butter and vanilla extract until light and fluffy, about 1 minute. Add the milk, cardamom, and cinnamon, and beat well. Reduce the speed to low and add the powdered sugar to reach desired consistency. Spread the icing on the cooled cookies.

Matt Boisen of Owatonna, Minnesota, found inspiration for these chewy, brightly flavored cookies after making a trip to Denmark during the holidays. "Cardamom and marzipan, they were the two things you smelled everywhere," he said. Later he ran across a recipe in a Danish cookbook that jogged two happy memories, recalling the frosted spice cookies that his aunt Beverly often made at the holidays and also reintroducing cardamom to his taste buds. "I know a lot of people run away from cardamom," said Boisen with a laugh. "But to me, it's intoxicating. I like to try something different. They're not like chocolate chip cookies. That's all my mom ever made, and I got burned out on them. No one can convince me to ever have another one of those."

CARDAMOM CRESCENTS

MAKES ABOUT 5 DOZEN COOKIES

Note: This dough must be prepared in advance.

- 1 teaspoon instant coffee
- 1 teaspoon ground cardamom
- ½ teaspoon baking powder
- 1¾ cups flour
- ½ cup (1 stick) unsalted butter, at room temperature
- 1 cup granulated sugar
- 2 cups finely ground hazelnuts or blanched almonds, divided
- 2 eggs
- 1 cup semisweet chocolate chips

In a medium bowl, whisk together the instant coffee, cardamom, baking powder, and flour, and reserve. In a bowl of an electric mixer on medium-high speed, beat the butter until creamy, about 1 minute. Add the granulated sugar and beat until light and fluffy, about 2 minutes. Add 1 cup of the ground hazelnuts or almonds and beat until thoroughly combined. Add the eggs, one at a time, beating well after each addition. Reduce the speed to low, add the flour mixture, and mix until just combined. Cover the bowl with plastic wrap and refrigerate for at least 1 hour.

When ready to bake, preheat the oven to 350°F and line the baking sheets with parchment paper. Form rounded teaspoons of dough into 2-inch crescent shapes and place 1 inch apart on the prepared baking sheets. Bake until the edges are golden brown, 12 to 15 minutes. Remove the cookies from the oven and cool for 2 minutes before transferring them to a wire rack to cool completely.

In a double boiler over gently simmering water (or in a bowl in a microwave oven), melt the chocolate and stir until very smooth. Quickly dip one end of each crescent into chocolate and then into the remaining 1 cup of chopped nuts. Transfer the cookies to wire racks over wax paper and cool until the chocolate sets.

Jingle bell season or not, there is always something delicious filling the cookie jar in Leslie Smith's kitchen in Minneapolis, Minnesota. "Cookies are my weakness," she said. In December, that means Cardamom Crescents. Smith ran across the recipe in a magazine and modified it to suit her family's tastes, jokingly labeling the not-so-sweet biscotti-like treat a "fusion" cookie. The cardamom recalls her and her husband's Scandinavian background and also reflects the Indian heritage of their three adopted children, who love to pitch in when she's baking. "They fight over who gets to help," she said. "They know that they get to sample."

CARDAMOM ORANGE ZEST SUGAR COOKIES

MAKES ABOUT 3 DOZEN COOKIES

Note: This dough must be prepared in advance. As the cookies cooled, we decorated with freshly grated orange zest, for additional flavor and color.

For cookies:

2 cups plus 2 tablespoons flour	½ cup powdered sugar
½ teaspoon salt	½ cup canola oil
½ teaspoon baking soda	1 egg
½ cup (1 stick) unsalted butter, at room temperature	½ teaspoon vanilla extract
	Freshly grated zest from 2 oranges
½ cup granulated sugar	1 teaspoon ground cardamom

For decoration:

1½ tablespoons granulated sugar	1 tablespoon unsalted butter, at room temperature
½ teaspoon ground cardamom	
	Freshly grated zest from 1 orange, optional

To prepare cookies: In a medium bowl, whisk together the flour, salt, and baking soda, and reserve. In a bowl of an electric mixer on medium-high speed, beat the butter, granulated sugar, and powdered sugar until light and fluffy, about 2 minutes. Add the canola oil, egg, vanilla extract, orange zest, and cardamom, and beat until thoroughly combined. Reduce the speed to low, add the flour mixture, and mix until just combined. Cover the bowl with plastic wrap and refrigerate for at least 1 hour. When ready to bake, preheat the oven to 350°F and line the baking sheets with parchment paper.

To decorate cookies: In a small bowl, stir together the granulated sugar and cardamom. Shape the dough into 1-inch balls and place 2 inches apart on the prepared baking sheets. Grease the bottom of a flat-bottomed glass with butter and dip it in the sugar–cardamom mixture; then carefully press the cookie with the flat bottom of the glass. Repeat with the remaining cookies. Bake until the bottom of the cookies are golden brown, about 10 to 12 minutes. Remove the cookies from the oven and cool for 2 minutes before transferring them to a wire rack to cool completely. Sprinkle with orange zest, if desired.

The roots for this easy-to-prepare recipe reach back to Jeanne Nordstrom's childhood in Wadena, Minnesota. "People would trade recipes, and a neighbor of ours had given this one to Mom," said Nordstrom, who now lives in St. Paul, Minnesota. "Mom made rolled-out sugar cookies, but I never got into that. These were much easier to make." The idea of infusing this beloved sugar cookie with cardamom and orange accents occurred to Nordstrom, and a taste test at a get-together of high school friends confirmed her suspicions. "I always bring cookies," she said. "They loved this updated version." Contest judges concurred. "It's a Christmas cookie that everyone will want to bake," said one. "It tastes like the holidays," added another. "It looks like a snickerdoodle, but then it has that surprise orange–cardamom flavor," observed a third.

CASHEW LEMON SHORTBREAD COOKIES

MAKES ABOUT 3 DOZEN COOKIES

1 cup (2 sticks) unsalted butter, at room temperature

¾ cup granulated sugar, divided

1 teaspoon lemon extract (or 1 teaspoon freshly squeezed lemon juice and lemon zest)

1 teaspoon vanilla extract

2 cups flour

½ cup roasted cashews, chopped

Freshly grated lemon zest, optional

Preheat the oven to 325°F and line the baking sheets with parchment paper. In a bowl of an electric mixer on medium-high speed, beat the butter until creamy, about 1 minute. Gradually add ½ cup granulated sugar and beat until light and fluffy, about 2 minutes. Add the lemon extract (or lemon juice and lemon zest) and vanilla extract, and beat until thoroughly combined. Reduce the speed to low, add the flour, and mix just until the dough begins to form a ball. Stir in the cashews.

Shape the dough into 1½-inch balls. Roll the dough balls in the remaining ¼ cup granulated sugar, place 2 inches apart on prepared baking sheets, and flatten with the bottom of a glass (and sprinkle with a bit of fresh lemon zest, if desired). Bake just until cookies are set and edges are lightly browned, 17 to 19 minutes. Remove the cookies from the oven and cool for 2 minutes before transferring them to a wire rack to cool completely.

Although Jean Livingood of Detroit Lakes, Minnesota, has been making Cashew Lemon Shortbread Cookies for a short time, they've hit number 1 on her family's cookie roster of greatest hits. Not just at Christmas, either. Her oldest daughter unearthed the recipe in an old cookbook, and everywhere she took them the reaction was the same: wow. At a recent birthday party, the shortbread was quickly reduced to a few crumbs, the only food item completely gone by the event's end. "That happens everywhere we take them," Livingood said. Besides their simple goodness and easy-to-follow instructions, there's another reason why Livingood has added these newcomers to her baking mix. "I'm a chocolate freak," she said. "And my daughters say, 'Mom, we can't make everything chocolate.'"

Every year, the roomy kitchen in Lisa Osacho's Eden Prairie, Minnesota, home becomes Christmas Cookie Baking Central, the place where her family gathers and bakes for the holidays. One favorite is a buttery, delicate-as-pie-crust delight from her mother's yuletide baking routine. Even a beloved family classic isn't off limits to Osacho's tinkering, this time involving a chai formula found in a magazine for Lunds & Byerlys supermarkets. "I like to read recipes and put a modern twist on them, make my own concoctions," she said. "You know what they remind me of?" asked one of our judges. "A really, really good version of pecan sandies. I always loved those cookies."

CHAI CRESCENTS
MAKES ABOUT 2 DOZEN COOKIES

Note: This dough must be prepared in advance. To toast pecans or walnuts, place the nuts in a dry skillet over medium heat and cook, stirring (or shaking the pan frequently), until they just begin to release their fragrance, about 3 to 4 minutes (alternately, preheat oven to 325°F, spread the nuts on an ungreased baking sheet, and bake, stirring often, for 4 to 6 minutes). Remove the nuts from the heat and cool to room temperature.

For cookies:

- ½ cup (1 stick) unsalted butter, at room temperature
- 3 tablespoons granulated sugar
- 1 cup flour, plus extra for rolling dough
- 1 teaspoon vanilla extract
- Pinch of salt
- ½ cup finely chopped toasted pecans or walnuts

For chai spice blend:

- ¼ teaspoon ground cloves
- ½ teaspoon ground cardamom
- ½ teaspoon ground ginger
- ¼ teaspoon ground white pepper
- ½ teaspoon ground cinnamon
- ⅔ cup superfine sugar

To prepare cookies: In a food processor fitted with a metal blade, combine the butter, granulated sugar, flour, vanilla extract, and salt, and pulse until combined. Transfer the dough to a large bowl and stir in the chopped nuts. Cover the bowl with plastic wrap and refrigerate at least 4 hours or overnight.

To prepare chai spice blend: In a small bowl, whisk together the cloves, cardamom, ginger, white pepper, cinnamon, and superfine sugar, and reserve.

When ready to bake, preheat the oven to 350°F and line the baking sheets with parchment paper. Remove the dough from the refrigerator and soften for 20 to 30 minutes. Form the dough into 1-inch balls. On a lightly floured work surface, roll the dough balls until the dough is shaped into finger-size sticks. Shape the sticks into crescents, place 1 inch apart on the prepared baking sheets, and bake until golden brown on the bottom, about 10 minutes. Remove the cookies from the oven and cool for 2 minutes before transferring them to a wire rack to cool for an additional 5 minutes. While they are still warm, carefully dip the cookies in the chai spice blend and transfer them to a wire rack over wax paper to cool completely.

ROLLED COOKIES

CHOCOLATE PEPPERMINT COOKIES

MAKES ABOUT 2 DOZEN COOKIES

For cookies:

1½ cups flour

½ cup unsweetened cocoa powder

¼ teaspoon salt

¼ teaspoon baking powder

¼ teaspoon baking soda

½ cup (1 stick) unsalted butter, at room temperature

1 cup granulated sugar

1 egg

1½ teaspoons vanilla extract

For topping:

3 tablespoons unsalted butter, at room temperature

2 cups powdered sugar

1 teaspoon peppermint extract

1 to 3 tablespoons milk (or heavy cream)

⅓ cup crushed hard peppermint candies (such as candy canes)

To prepare cookies: Preheat the oven to 350°F and line the baking sheets with parchment paper. In a medium bowl, whisk together the flour, cocoa, salt, baking powder, and baking soda, and reserve.

In a bowl of an electric mixer on medium-high speed, beat the butter until creamy, about 1 minute. Add the granulated sugar and beat until light and fluffy, about 2 minutes. Add the egg and vanilla extract, and beat until thoroughly combined. Reduce the speed to low, add the flour mixture, and mix until just combined.

Shape the dough into 1-inch balls and place 2 inches apart on the prepared baking sheets, flattening the dough slightly. Bake until the cookies are set and dry-looking, about 10 minutes. Remove the cookies from the oven and cool for 2 minutes before transferring them to a wire rack to cool completely.

To prepare topping: In a bowl of an electric mixer on medium speed, combine the butter and powdered sugar, and beat until creamy. Add the peppermint extract and enough milk (or cream), 1 tablespoon at a time, to achieve a smooth mixture. Spread the icing on the cooled cookies; then press the cookie top into the crushed candy.

For years, Karen Evans of Minneapolis, Minnesota, has been baking gigantic amounts of holiday cookies as a gift-giving gesture for her husband's coworkers. After all, "Who doesn't like homemade cookies?" she said. "Every year I try to bake a couple of new kinds, to add to the old favorites." Evans began making this festive cookie—a variation on a recipe she encountered in the pages of the *Cincinnati Enquirer*—more than twenty years ago. It quickly became her family's "all-time favorite." Our judges agreed. "Kids are going to love this," was the near-unanimous chorus of praise. Evans values finicky-free recipes. "These cookies look sophisticated, but they're actually really easy to make," she said. "And if there are any flaws, you're going to cover them in icing and roll them in crushed candy canes."

CRANBERRY CAT KISSES

MAKES ABOUT 4 DOZEN COOKIES

For cookies:

- 1 **cup (2 sticks) unsalted butter, at room temperature**
- ½ **cup powdered sugar**
- ½ **teaspoon almond extract**
- 2¼ **cups flour**
- ¾ **cup finely chopped almonds**
- ½ **cup dried cranberries, finely chopped**

For chocolate coating:

- 1 **cup semisweet chocolate chips**
- 2 **tablespoons shortening**
- **Sliced almonds for decoration**

To prepare cookies: Preheat the oven to 400°F and line the baking sheets with parchment paper. In a bowl using an electric mixer on medium-high speed, beat the butter until creamy, about 1 minute. Add the powdered sugar and beat until light and fluffy, about 2 minutes. Add the almond extract and beat until thoroughly combined. Reduce the speed to low, add the flour and mix until just combined. Stir in the almonds and dried cranberries.

Shape the dough into 1-inch balls and place 2 inches apart on the prepared baking sheets. Bake until the cookies are set but not browned, 7 to 8 minutes. Remove the cookies from the oven and cool for 5 minutes before transferring them to a wire rack to cool completely.

To prepare chocolate coating: In a double boiler over gently simmering water (or in a bowl in a microwave oven), melt the chocolate chips and shortening, whisking until combined. Dip the top of the cooled cookies in the melted chocolate, decorate with an almond slice, and transfer to wax paper until the chocolate sets.

Anne Park and her daughter Hannah Park, both of St. Paul, Minnesota, created this recipe while driving in the car. Well, at least the idea for it. "We were talking about what makes a good holiday cookie," said Anne. "My contribution was chocolate." And Hannah? Cranberries. "I really like Craisins," she said, referring to dried cranberries. "Mom was convinced that cherries would be better, but I knew cranberries would be better." Back in their St. Paul kitchen, they borrowed ideas from other favorite cookies: the taste of butter from spritz, an egg-free formula from Russian tea cakes ("So we could bake without having any eggs in the house," said Anne), and a chocolate-dipped coating from peanut butter balls. Cat Kisses (a nod to the family feline, Neko) was an immediate hit. Just another day's work for the mother–daughter team.

ESPRESSO–HAZELNUT TRUFFLE COOKIES

MAKES ABOUT 3 DOZEN COOKIES

Note: This dough must be prepared in advance.

For cookies:

4 ounces unsweetened chocolate	2 tablespoons unsweetened cocoa powder
1¼ cup semisweet mini–chocolate chips, divided	¼ teaspoon baking powder
2 teaspoons instant espresso powder	¼ teaspoon salt
⅓ cup (5⅓ tablespoons) unsalted butter, at room temperature	1 cup granulated sugar
¾ cup flour	3 eggs
	¼ cup finely chopped hazelnuts

For glaze:

⅓ cup semisweet mini–chocolate chips	¼ cup finely chopped hazelnuts
1 tablespoon vegetable oil	

To prepare cookies: In a double boiler over gently simmering water (or in a bowl in a microwave oven), melt the unsweetened chocolate, 1 cup chocolate chips, instant espresso powder, and butter, whisking until smooth. Remove the chocolate mixture from the heat and cool for 10 minutes.

In a medium bowl, whisk together the flour, cocoa, baking powder, and salt, and reserve. In a bowl of an electric mixer on medium-high speed, beat the granulated sugar and eggs until light and fluffy, about 2 minutes. Add the chocolate mixture and beat until thoroughly combined. Reduce the speed to low, add the flour mixture, and mix until combined. Stir in the remaining ¼ cup chocolate chips and the hazelnuts. Cover the bowl with plastic wrap and refrigerate for at least 6 hours or overnight.

When ready to bake, preheat the oven to 350°F and line the baking sheets with parchment paper. Shape the dough into 1-inch balls and place 2 inches apart on the prepared baking sheets, flattening the dough slightly. Bake until lightly puffed and just set, about 9 to 11 minutes. Remove the cookies from the oven and cool for 2 minutes before transferring them to a wire rack to cool completely.

To prepare glaze: In a double boiler over gently simmering water (or in a bowl in a microwave oven), melt the chocolate chips and vegetable oil, stirring to combine. Drizzle the chocolate over the cooled cookies; sprinkle with the chopped hazelnuts. Allow the glaze to set.

Why chocolate? That's easy. "My kids are chocoholics," said Cheryl Francke of Arden Hills, Minnesota, who also observed that any chocolate dessert on her sprawling Thanksgiving buffet that includes the word "truffle" in its name always disappears quickly. "I have a chocolate-truffle torte and I thought, 'Maybe I could make a cookie that comes close to that,'" she said. Our judges were instantly smitten. "It's intense, in a good way," said one. "It's the grown-up version of that popular chocolate–peppermint cookie," said another. There was no hesitation when Francke was asked about the one baking tool she couldn't live without. "My mixer," she said. "I have a KitchenAid, and it's the greatest thing in the world. I don't think there is a week that goes by that I'm not using it. There's always something going on in that kitchen."

FRENCH–SWISS BUTTER COOKIES
MAKES ABOUT 5 DOZEN COOKIES

Note: This dough must be prepared in advance.

1 cup (2 sticks) unsalted butter, at room
   temperature
1 cup granulated sugar
1 egg, separated

2½ teaspoons ground cinnamon
2 cups flour, plus extra for pressing dough
   Finely chopped walnuts (or pecans or
   decorative sugar)

In a bowl of an electric mixer on medium-high speed, beat the butter until creamy, about 1 minute. Gradually add the granulated sugar and beat until light and fluffy, about 2 minutes. Add the egg yolk and beat until thoroughly combined. Reduce the speed to low, add the cinnamon and flour, and mix until just combined. Cover the bowl with plastic wrap and refrigerate for at least 1 hour.

When ready to bake, preheat the oven to 350°F and line the baking sheets with parchment paper. In a small bowl, slightly beat the reserved egg white with a fork. Shape the dough into small balls and place 2 inches apart on the prepared baking sheets. Dip a flat-bottomed glass in flour and press dough to ¹⁄₁₆- to ⅛-inch thickness, re-flouring the glass with each cookie.

Brush a little egg white in the center of each cookie; then sprinkle the center with chopped walnuts (or pecans or decorative sugar). Bake 10 to 12 minutes; do not overbake. Remove the cookies from the oven and cool for 2 minutes before transferring them to a wire rack to cool completely.

Years ago, Ramona Doebler of Elk River, Minnesota, asked her mother to share a cherished recipe, a cinnamon-flavored sugar cookie. "But she couldn't find it," said Doebler. "So I sent a request into the newspaper," she said, referring to the then-new Taste section of the *Star Tribune* and its instantly popular Reader's Exchange feature. Doebler still has the handwritten response, and the recipe. "I saw your request for cookies in today's paper," wrote Doebler's cookie guardian angel, otherwise known as Myrtle Eveland of Anoka, Minnesota. "I'm sure this is the one you want—so I'll send it directly to you. I hope you like them as well as I do."

HOT AND SASSY PEANUT BUTTER BUDS

MAKES ABOUT 3 DOZEN COOKIES

Note: This dough must be prepared in advance. Two options for chocolate bars are Chuao Chocolatier's Spicy Maya or Lindt's Excellence Chili.

1¼ cups flour	⅓ cup (5⅓ tablespoons) unsalted butter, at room temperature
1 teaspoon baking soda	
½ teaspoon salt	½ cup firmly packed brown sugar
¼ teaspoon plus ⅛ teaspoon cayenne pepper, divided	1 egg
	1 teaspoon vanilla extract
¼ teaspoon freshly ground nutmeg	¼ cup granulated sugar
2 tablespoons sesame seeds	3 ounces dark chocolate bar infused with chile
½ cup crunchy peanut butter, at room temperature	¼ cup semisweet chocolate chips
	3 ounces white chocolate

In a medium bowl, whisk together the flour, baking soda, salt, ¼ teaspoon cayenne pepper, nutmeg, and sesame seeds, and reserve.

In a bowl of an electric mixer on medium-high speed, beat the peanut butter and butter until creamy, about 1 minute. Add the brown sugar and beat until light and fluffy, about 2 minutes. Add the egg and vanilla extract, and beat until fully combined. Reduce the speed to low, add the flour mixture, a third at a time, and mix until thoroughly combined. Cover the bowl with plastic wrap and refrigerate overnight or up to 2 days.

When ready to bake, preheat the oven to 350°F and line the baking sheets with parchment paper. In a small bowl, whisk together the granulated sugar and the remaining ⅛ teaspoon cayenne pepper. Shape the dough into 1-inch balls. Roll the dough balls in the sugar–cayenne pepper mixture and place 2 inches apart on the prepared baking sheets. Bake until slightly browned, 10 to 12 minutes. Remove the cookies from the oven and cool for 5 minutes before transferring them to a wire rack to cool completely.

In a double boiler over gently simmering water (or in a bowl in a microwave oven), melt the dark chocolate bar and chocolate chips, stirring until smooth. Dip the tops of the cooled cookies into the melted chocolate and place on wax paper to set. In a double boiler over simmering water, melt the white chocolate. Drizzle the white chocolate over the cookies.

Janet Heirigs of Minneapolis, Minnesota, admitted that she's not much of a Christmas cookie baker, although she usually makes these spicy treats, along with cranberry biscotti and rum balls. "I usually start with the rum balls," she said with a laugh. The recipe began with good intentions, for a cookie. "When my kids were little, I was trying to feed them only wholesome things, and I found a recipe in Jane Brody's 1985 *Good Food* cookbook," she said. "It was called 'Peanut Butter Rounds,' and it was a boost of protein for my skinny little boys." All these years later, Heirigs has baked—and altered—the recipe so often "that it's never the same way twice," she said. That includes the eureka moment when she thought to add cayenne pepper. "Now they give you that nice, warm feeling," she said.

HOT COCOA COOKIES
MAKES 2 TO 3 DOZEN COOKIES

Note: This dough must be prepared in advance. Mini-marshmallows could be substituted for the larger size. Feel free to experiment with the type of chocolate in this intensely chocolaty cookie. While the recipe calls for semisweet, a mix of bittersweet (chopped and melted for the dough) and semisweet (for the pieces under the marshmallow) is also a delicious combination.

1½ **cups flour**	½ **cup (1 stick) unsalted butter**
¼ **cup unsweetened cocoa powder**	1¼ **cups light brown sugar**
1½ **teaspoons baking powder**	3 **eggs**
¼ **teaspoon salt**	1½ **teaspoons vanilla extract**
16 **ounces semisweet chocolate, divided**	30 **marshmallows**

In a large bowl, whisk together the flour, cocoa powder, baking powder, and salt, and reserve. Chop 12 ounces of semisweet chocolate into ½-inch pieces. In a double boiler over gently simmering water (or in a bowl in a microwave oven), melt the butter and chopped chocolate, whisking frequently until smooth. Remove from the heat and cool for 15 minutes.

In a bowl of an electric mixer on medium speed, beat the sugar, eggs, and vanilla extract until smooth, about 2 minutes. Add the melted chocolate mixture and beat until just blended. Reduce the speed to low and add the flour mixture in two batches, mixing until just combined. Cover the bowl with plastic wrap and refrigerate for at least 1 hour.

When ready to bake, preheat the oven to 325°F and line the baking sheets with parchment paper. Break the remaining 4 ounces of chocolate into small pieces, and cut marshmallows (if necessary) into a size suitable for the top of the cookie. Shape the dough into 1-inch balls and place 2 inches apart on the prepared baking sheets, flattening the dough slightly. Bake until the tops of the cookies crack, about 12 minutes.

Remove the cookies from the oven and gently press a chocolate piece, then a marshmallow, into each cookie. Return them to the oven and bake until the marshmallows are just softened, about 4 minutes. Remove the cookies from the oven and cool for 5 minutes before transferring them to a wire rack. Grate remaining chocolate over the warm cookies as a garnish, and cool completely.

Macy Hennen of Pierz, Minnesota, discovered this recipe online several years ago, although she can't recall the source. (We tracked a version of it to rachaelraymag.com.) No matter, because Hot Cocoa Cookies quickly earned a cherished position in the Hennen household's annual all-family December Eve cook- and bake-a-thon. And not only because they taste great. "It's a fun recipe to make," Hennen wrote in her entry. "These cookies get everyone in the Christmas mood." One judge noted, "Kids would like to make these." Another added: "And eat these."

ITALIAN ALMOND COOKIES

MAKES ABOUT 2 DOZEN COOKIES

1 **egg white**	⅛ **teaspoon honey**
2¼ **cups almond flour**	1 **teaspoon almond extract**
¾ **cups granulated sugar**	1 **teaspoon vanilla extract**
Zest of 1 large lemon	**Powdered sugar, for coating**

Preheat the oven to 350°F and line the baking sheets with parchment paper. In a bowl of an electric mixer on medium-high speed, beat the egg white until soft peaks form.

In a medium bowl, whisk together the almond flour, granulated sugar, and lemon zest. Stir in the egg white, honey, almond extract, and vanilla extract, and knead into a ball of dough (the dough will be slightly sticky). Shape the dough into a log about 1 inch in diameter. Using a sharp knife, cut the log at ½-inch intervals and form the dough into egg-shaped cookies.

Fill a shallow bowl with powdered sugar. Roll the cookies in the powdered sugar, coating all sides and gently tapping off excess powdered sugar. Place the cookies 1 inch apart on prepared baking sheets (cookies spread only slightly) and bake until only slightly browned with a cracked exterior, about 15 to 20 minutes. Do not overbake. Remove the cookies from the oven and cool for 5 minutes before transferring them to a wire rack to cool completely.

During a college study-abroad year at the Università di Bologna, William Teresa of Minneapolis, Minnesota, dated a fellow student. The couple would frequently visit her family in Cesena, a small city in Emilia–Romagna, where Teresa became immersed in the cooking lives of his girlfriend's parents and grandparents. "They were so lovely," he said. "It was wonderful to be in a place where food is so rooted in tradition and place, and to encounter something that has always been made by the same people, with little variation." One of the grandmothers baked a chewy-crispy and outrageously rich almond cookie, which the family enjoyed with espresso. Teresa was instantly smitten and perfected the formula when he returned home. "They're not like any other American cookie," he said. "Maybe that's why so many people ask me for the recipe."

LIME COOLERS
MAKES ABOUT 2 DOZEN COOKIES

Note: This dough must be prepared in advance. Since these cookies go fast and are a snap to make, you might as well double the recipe!

For cookies:

1 cup (2 sticks) unsalted butter, at room temperature, plus extra for flattening dough	¼ cup cornstarch
½ cup powdered sugar	1 tablespoon finely grated lime zest
1¾ cups flour	½ teaspoon vanilla extract
	Granulated sugar for flattening dough

For lime glaze:

½ cup powdered sugar	4 teaspoons freshly squeezed lime juice
2 to 3 teaspoons finely grated lime zest	

To prepare cookies: In a bowl of an electric mixer on medium-high speed, beat the butter until creamy, about 1 minute. Add the powdered sugar and beat until light and fluffy, about 2 minutes. Reduce the speed to low and add the flour, cornstarch, lime zest, and vanilla extract, and mix until just combined. Cover the bowl with plastic wrap and refrigerate for at least 1 hour.

When ready to bake, preheat the oven to 350°F and line the baking sheets with parchment paper. Shape the dough into 1-inch balls and place about 2 inches apart on the prepared baking sheets. Grease the bottom of a large flat glass with butter, press into granulated sugar, and gently press the glass on the cookies until the dough is about ¼ inch thick. Repeat, pressing the glass into the granulated sugar each time, until all the cookies are flattened. Bake until the edges are light golden brown, 9 to 11 minutes. Remove the cookies from the oven and cool for 2 minutes before transferring them to a wire rack to cool completely.

To prepare lime glaze: In a small bowl, whisk together the powdered sugar, lime zest, and lime juice until a light glaze forms. Using a knife, spread glaze across the cooled cookies.

One day at the supermarket, Stacy McNabb of Richfield, Minnesota, spied a lime cookie recipe in a cooking magazine. She was intrigued and gave it a shot. Talk about a runaway hit. "If I put it on a tray, it's the one recipe that everyone wants—every time," she said. There's plenty to this cookie's curb appeal: tart citrus, a festive green tint, and a light bite. "I don't like those heavily chocolate, super-sweet cookies," McNabb said. "There are already so many of those."

LIMONCELLO KISSES
MAKES ABOUT 4 DOZEN COOKIES

Note: Limoncello is an Italian lemon liqueur. If you don't want to use an alcoholic beverage as an ingredient, substitute cream or milk in the frosting (do not substitute lemon juice, as it will be too tart).

For cookies:

- 2 cups flour
- 1 teaspoon baking powder
- ½ teaspoon salt
- ¼ teaspoon baking soda
- 1½ cup granulated sugar
- 1 tablespoon freshly grated lemon zest

- ½ cup (1 stick) unsalted butter, at room temperature
- 1 egg
- 1 teaspoon vanilla extract
- 1 tablespoon freshly squeezed lemon juice
- ¼ cup sour cream

For frosting:

- 2 cup powdered sugar
- 3 tablespoons limoncello (see Note)
- 1 tablespoon freshly squeezed lemon juice

- Candied lemon slices, freshly grated lemon zest, or sprinkles, optional

To prepare cookies: Preheat the oven to 350°F and line the baking sheets with parchment paper. In a large bowl, whisk together the flour, baking powder, salt, and baking soda, and reserve.

In a medium bowl, combine the granulated sugar and lemon zest. Using your fingers, rub the zest into the sugar until fragrant, about 30 seconds.

In a bowl of an electric mixer on medium-high speed, beat the butter until creamy, about 1 minute. Add the lemon sugar and beat until light and fluffy, about 2 minutes. Add the egg, vanilla extract, and lemon juice, and beat until thoroughly combined. Reduce the speed to low and add the flour mixture by halves, alternating with the sour cream, and mix until just combined.

Shape the dough into 1-inch balls and place 2 inches apart on the prepared baking sheets. Bake until the cookies are just firm and the tops are barely beginning to brown, about 10 to 12 minutes. Remove the cookies from the oven and cool for 2 minutes before transferring them to a wire rack to cool completely.

To prepare frosting: In a medium bowl, whisk together the powdered sugar, limoncello, and lemon juice. Add more powdered sugar or lemon juice, as necessary, to achieve the desired consistency. Frost the top of each cooled cookie (or drizzle frosting over it). Place on a wire rack for the frosting to set. If desired, top each cookie with a candied lemon slice, freshly grated lemon zest, or holiday sprinkles.

For Joanne Holtmeier of Edina, Minnesota, adding lemon to her go-to sugar cookie recipe—she found it in *Everyday Food* magazine—was a no-brainer. "Everything citrus is my favorite," she said. "It balances out the sweetness of some of the other holiday flavors." Dialing up the flavor with limoncello was an idea inspired by her penchant for throwing cocktail parties. "I've purchased so many different liquors and liqueurs over the years, and I got to wondering how I could incorporate them into my baking," she said. "I love baking cookies, that's my hobby. Cookies make people happy. In moderation, of course."

"Every Christmas, I try to invent a new cookie," said Joan Hause of Lake Elmo, Minnesota. "I am the auntie who brings the platter full of goodies—the fudge, the spritz, the sugar cookie, along with a new creation." That drive to innovate was tapped as she was enjoying a cappuccino. "I looked at the swirly top and started thinking that it might be kind of pretty in a cookie," she said. "I've never made a cookie with coffee in it before. And I do like frosting." Our judges do, too. "This is the first cookie that anyone would reach for on a cookie platter," said one. "Look how pretty this is," added another.

MOCHA CAPPUCCINO COOKIES
MAKES ABOUT 4 DOZEN COOKIES

Note: This cookie has two types of frosting for added effect.

For cookies:

⅔ cup unsweetened cocoa powder	1 cup (2 sticks) unsalted butter, at room temperature
½ teaspoon salt	
2 teaspoons granulated fine-ground espresso or dark roast coffee	1⅓ cup granulated sugar
	2 egg yolks
2 cups flour	¼ cup milk
	2 teaspoons vanilla extract

For the frostings:

½ cup (1 stick) unsalted butter, at room temperature	1 teaspoon vanilla extract
	3 ounces white chocolate
1¼ cup powdered sugar	3 ounces bittersweet chocolate

To prepare cookies: Preheat the oven to 350°F and line the baking sheets with parchment paper. In a large bowl, whisk together the cocoa powder, salt, espresso (or coffee), and flour, and reserve.

In a bowl of an electric mixer on medium-high speed, beat the butter until creamy, about 1 minute. Add the granulated sugar and beat until light and fluffy, about 2 minutes. Add the egg yolks, milk, and vanilla extract, and beat until thoroughly combined. Reduce the speed to low, slowly add the flour mixture, and mix until just combined.

Shape the dough into 1½-inch balls and place 2 inches apart on prepared baking sheets. Using a wide-bottomed glass, carefully press the dough to ½-inch thickness before baking. Bake until the cookies are set and the tops are dry, about 8 to 9 minutes. Remove the cookies from the oven and cool for 2 minutes before transferring them to a wire rack to cool completely.

To prepare frostings: In a double boiler over gently simmering water (or in a bowl in a microwave oven), melt the white chocolate, whisking occasionally. Melt the bittersweet chocolate in the same manner. Allow the chocolate to cool slightly.

In a bowl of an electric mixer on medium-high speed, beat the butter until creamy, about 1 minute. Reduce the speed to medium-low and add the powdered sugar and vanilla extract, and mix until creamy. Divide the frosting into two bowls. Add the melted white chocolate to one bowl and the melted bittersweet chocolate to the other, stirring until thoroughly combined. If either frosting needs to be thicker, add more powdered sugar.

Using a frosting gun, fill the container with alternating spoonsful of white chocolate frosting and bittersweet chocolate frosting. Create a white chocolate / bittersweet chocolate swirl on top of each cookie, about 2 teaspoons per cookie; a medium-size star tip works well. If using a pastry bag, use a coupler that allows you to attach 2 pastry bags, one for each frosting. The same effect can be made by placing 1 teaspoon of each icing on top of a cookie and swirling the frosting with a butter knife.

NUT GOODIE THUMBPRINTS

MAKES ABOUT 2 DOZEN COOKIES

Note: This dough must be prepared in advance.

For cookies:

1 cup flour	⅔ cup packed light brown sugar
⅓ cup unsweetened cocoa powder	1 egg, separated
¼ teaspoon salt	2 tablespoons whole milk
½ cup (1 stick) unsalted butter, at room temperature	2 teaspoons vanilla extract
	¾ cup chopped roasted and salted peanuts

For filling:

2 tablespoons unsalted butter, at room temperature	½ teaspoon vanilla extract
2 tablespoons sweetened condensed milk	1½ teaspoons whole milk
1 teaspoon maple extract	1 cup powdered sugar

For ganache:

½ cup semisweet chocolate chips	2 tablespoons heavy cream

To prepare cookies: In a medium bowl, whisk together the flour, cocoa powder, and salt, and reserve. In a bowl of a mixer on medium-high speed, beat together the butter and brown sugar until light and fluffy, about 2 minutes. Add the egg yolk, milk, and vanilla extract, and beat until thoroughly combined. Reduce the speed to low, gradually add the flour mixture, and mix just until combined. Form the dough into a disk, wrap in plastic wrap, and refrigerate for at least 30 minutes.

When ready to bake, preheat the oven to 350°F and line the baking sheets with parchment paper. Shape the dough into 1-inch balls. Dip the top half of each ball into the egg white and then into the peanuts. Place the dough, peanuts-side up, 2 inches apart on the prepared baking sheets. Using the back of a spoon or your thumb, press an indentation into the center of each cookie. Bake until the cookies are set but still soft, about 10 to 12 minutes. Remove the cookies from the oven and carefully remake the same slight indentation into the top of each cookie. Cool for 5 minutes before transferring the cookies to a wire rack to cool completely.

To prepare filling: In a bowl of an electric mixer on medium speed, combine the butter, condensed milk, maple extract, vanilla extract, whole milk, and powdered sugar, and beat until uniform and creamy. While the cookies are still slightly warm, spoon the filling into the indentation in the cookies; then allow them to cool completely.

To prepare ganache: In a double boiler over gently simmering water (or in a bowl in a microwave oven), melt the chocolate and cream, stirring until smooth. Use the tines of a fork to drizzle the chocolate over the cooled cookies. Allow the ganache to set before serving.

Crystal Schlueter of Babbitt, Minnesota, is nutty about Nut Goodies: "I've always been a fan," she said. "In the checkout line at the grocery store, Mom would let me buy a candy bar, and it was always the one I'd choose. Of course, it's a Minnesota classic." It sure is: Pearson Candy Company in St. Paul has been producing the chocolate–maple–peanut confection since 1912. For her candy bar–inspired recipe, Schlueter deviated slightly from the original, replacing milk chocolate with semisweet. Another alteration from the Pearson's formula is the inclusion of salted peanuts. "I like the fact that the cookie is chewy and crispy, and that very sweet maple filling is different from the crunchy, salty peanuts," said Schlueter. "That's a combination a lot of people like."

While conducting research on Swedish immigrant food traditions, Patrice Johnson of Roseville, Minnesota, was told by an elderly woman that she had to try the cookie called Melting Moments. "I learned that these cookies used to be as popular as chocolate chip cookies are today," said Johnson. One slight hitch, however: "I haven't found any evidence that it's a Scandinavian cookie," she said with a laugh. "But I love that it's so simple, just five ingredients—and you always have them on hand—and some kind of flavoring." After tinkering with the recipe, she decided to enter a lemon–basil variation in the Minnesota State Fair's baking competition. The humid weather had other ideas, and Johnson went back to the drawing board, this time looking back on the Danish pastries her mother baked on Christmas morning. Bingo.

ORANGE–ALMOND MELTING MOMENTS

MAKES ABOUT 2 DOZEN COOKIES

Note: This dough must be prepared in advance.

For cookies:

1 **cup flour**

⅔ **cup cornstarch**

¼ **teaspoon ground cayenne pepper**

¼ **teaspoon salt**

1 **cup (2 sticks) unsalted butter, cut into tablespoons, at room temperature**

⅓ **cup powdered sugar**

Freshly grated zest of 1 orange

½ **teaspoon almond extract**

For icing:

3 **tablespoons freshly squeezed orange juice**

1 **tablespoon unsalted butter, at room temperature**

1 **teaspoon almond extract**

1 **teaspoon vanilla extract**

¼ **teaspoon salt**

2¾ **cups powdered sugar**

½ **cup raw sliced almonds for garnish**

Freshly grated orange zest for garnish, optional

To prepare cookies: In a large bowl, whisk together the flour, cornstarch, cayenne pepper, and salt, and reserve. In a bowl of an electric mixer on medium-high speed, beat the butter until creamy, about 1 minute. Add the powdered sugar, orange zest, and almond extract, and beat until light and fluffy, about 2 minutes. Reduce the speed to low, add the flour mixture, and mix until a grainy dough forms. Use your hands to shape the dough into a round ball. Wrap the dough in plastic wrap and refrigerate for 30 to 60 minutes.

When ready to bake, preheat the oven to 325°F and line the baking sheets with parchment paper. Shape the dough into tablespoon-sized balls and place 2 inches apart on the prepared baking sheets. Bake 12 to 14 minutes (the cookies will be very light-colored); do not overbake. Remove the cookies from the oven and cool for 5 minutes before transferring them to a wire rack to cool completely.

To prepare icing: In a bowl of an electric mixer on medium speed, beat the orange juice, butter, almond extract, vanilla extract, and salt until creamy, about 1 minute. Reduce the speed to low, add the powdered sugar, and mix until smooth. Using a small spatula or knife (or a pastry bag), ice the cookies. For a less sweet cookie, use only 1 teaspoon icing per cookie; for a sweeter cookie, frost liberally with the icing. Garnish with almonds and orange zest, if desired.

ROLLED COOKIES

ORANGE GINGER DROPS

MAKES ABOUT 4 DOZEN COOKIES

Note: This dough must be prepared in advance.

2¼ cups flour

2 teaspoons baking soda

¼ teaspoon salt

½ teaspoon ground cloves

1 teaspoon ground cinnamon

1 teaspoon ground ginger

1 tablespoon plus 2 teaspoons freshly grated orange zest, divided

1 tablespoon chopped crystallized ginger, plus extra for garnish

¾ cup (1½ sticks) unsalted butter, at room temperature

1 cup packed brown sugar

1 egg

¼ cup molasses

1 tablespoon freshly squeezed orange juice

3 tablespoons granulated sugar

In a large bowl, whisk together the flour, baking soda, salt, cloves, cinnamon, ground ginger, 1 tablespoon orange zest, and crystallized ginger, and reserve. In a bowl of an electric mixer on medium-high speed, beat the butter and brown sugar until creamy, about 1 minute. Add the egg, molasses, and orange juice, and beat until thoroughly combined. Reduce the speed to low, add the flour mixture, and mix until just combined. Cover the bowl with plastic wrap and refrigerate for at least 1 hour.

Meanwhile, in a small bowl, combine the remaining 2 teaspoons orange zest with granulated sugar. Using your fingers, blend the mixture thoroughly until the orange zest has a crystallized appearance and texture, and reserve.

When ready to bake, preheat the oven to 375°F and line the baking sheets with parchment paper. Shape the dough into 1¼-inch balls. Dip the dough balls in the orange zest mixture and place, sugar-side up, 2 inches apart on the prepared baking sheets. Press a few pieces of the crystallized ginger into the sugared top. Bake until the cookies are set but not hard, 10 to 12 minutes. Remove the cookies from the oven and cool for 2 minutes before transferring them to a wire rack to cool completely.

"I associate the taste of ginger with this time of year," said Cheryl Francke of Arden Hills, Minnesota. "Whether it's gingerbread men, or gingersnaps, it's very reminiscent of the holidays. I've always had at least one ginger cookie combined into my holiday baking." She's constantly baking ("After a full day's work, you'll find me in the kitchen," she said), and twisting old flavors. "I thought I would experiment with crystallized ginger and see what I could come up with; then I thought that orange would be a nice complement," she said. "It's good to know that playing in the kitchen pays off once in a while." That crystallized ginger–orange garnish is there for more than just flavor. "I think things taste better if they look better," she said. "I bake a lot of muffins, and I always like to top them with something, so when you look at them you know what you're biting into."

PERSIAN MOLASSES CRINKLES
MAKES ABOUT 3 DOZEN COOKIES

Note: Find pomegranate molasses in Middle Eastern specialty stores or in the imported foods sections of most supermarkets. To make your own, combine 4 cups pomegranate juice, ½ cup granulated sugar, and 1 tablespoon freshly squeezed lemon juice in a medium saucepan; cook over medium heat, stirring, until the granulated sugar dissolves. Reduce the heat to medium-low and cook until the mixture reduces to 1 cup and is the consistency of thick syrup, about 75 minutes. Remove the pan from the heat, cool for 30 minutes, and transfer to an uncovered glass jar to cool completely. To toast slivered almonds, place the nuts in a dry skillet over medium heat and cook, stirring or shaking the pan frequently, until they just begin to release their fragrance, about 3 to 4 minutes (alternately, preheat the oven to 325°F, spread the nuts on an ungreased baking sheet, and bake, stirring often, for 4 to 6 minutes). Remove the nuts from the heat and cool to room temperature. For best results with this recipe, beat the butter and sugar for a long time.

2½ cups flour	6 tablespoons pomegranate molasses (see Note)
2 teaspoons baking soda	
¼ teaspoon salt	2 teaspoons freshly grated lemon zest
¾ cup shortening	1 egg
1 cup granulated sugar	¾ cup slivered almonds, toasted and very finely chopped

Preheat the oven to 350°F and line the baking sheets with parchment paper. In a medium bowl, whisk together the flour, baking soda, and salt, and reserve.

In a bowl of an electric mixer on medium-high speed, beat the shortening and granulated sugar until light and fluffy, about 2 minutes. Add the pomegranate molasses and lemon zest, and beat until thoroughly combined. Add the egg and beat until thoroughly combined. Reduce the speed to low, add the flour mixture, and mix until just combined (the dough will be soft).

Shape the dough into 1-inch balls. Dip the dough into the chopped almonds and place 2 inches apart on the prepared baking sheets, almond-side up. Bake until the cookies are puffed and deeply cracked, 10 to 12 minutes. Remove the cookies from the oven and cool for 2 minutes before transferring them to a wire rack to cool completely.

ROLLED COOKIES

137

A trip to Turkey proved inspirational for Lance Swanson of North Branch, Minnesota. "I fell in love with some of the flavors over there, and when I came home I started trying to re-create them," he said. "I saw the bottle of pomegranate molasses that was just sitting on our shelf and I thought, 'Why not replace regular molasses with it?' After a lot of trial and error, the results really brought me back to Turkey." Swanson is pleased with how easy these cookies are to prepare. "You mix, you scoop, you bake," he said. "That's it."

PISTACHIO ORANGE COOKIES

MAKES ABOUT 3 DOZEN SANDWICH COOKIES

For cookies:

- 2 **cups flour**
- 1 **teaspoon salt**
- 2 **teaspoons cream of tartar**
- 1 **teaspoon baking soda**
- 1 **cup (2 sticks) unsalted butter, at room temperature**
- ½ **cup granulated sugar, plus extra for rolling dough**
- ½ **cup firmly packed brown sugar**
- 1 **egg**
- 1 **teaspoon vanilla extract**

For filling:

- 1 **cup raw shelled pistachios, divided**
- ½ **cup (1 stick) unsalted butter, at room temperature**
- **Freshly grated zest of 1 orange, finely chopped**
- 1 **teaspoon orange extract**
- 1 **teaspoon vanilla extract**
- 3 **cups powdered sugar**
- 2 **tablespoons milk (or use 1 tablespoon milk and 1 tablespoon freshly squeezed orange juice)**

To prepare cookies: Preheat the oven to 350°F and line the baking sheets with parchment paper. In a large bowl, whisk together the flour, salt, cream of tartar, and baking soda, and reserve.

In a bowl of an electric mixer on medium-high speed, beat the butter, granulated sugar, and brown sugar until light and fluffy, about 2 minutes. Add the egg and vanilla extract and beat until thoroughly combined. Reduce the speed to low and add the flour mixture, in thirds, mixing until just combined.

Shape the dough into ½-inch balls (about the size of a chestnut). Roll the dough in granulated sugar and place 2 inches apart on the prepared baking sheets. Bake until the cookies are set but not browned, about 11 minutes (the cookies will puff up in the oven, but then flatten). Remove the cookies from the oven and cool for 2 minutes before transferring them to a wire rack to cool completely.

To prepare filling: In a food processor fitted with a metal blade, pulse ½ cup pistachios until very fine (the nuts should almost clump together in a paste between your fingers), and reserve.

In a bowl of an electric mixer on medium-high speed, beat the butter with the orange zest until creamy, about 1 minute. Add the orange extract and vanilla extract, and beat until thoroughly combined. Reduce the speed to low and add the powdered sugar, in thirds, alternating with the milk (or milk and orange juice), beginning and ending with powdered sugar, and mix until smooth (you may need another tablespoon or so of liquid to reach the desired consistency). Fold in the chopped pistachios and mix until thoroughly combined.

To assemble cookies: Finely chop the remaining ½ cup pistachios and place in a shallow dish. Spread a generous dollop of the filling on the flat side of one cookie. Place the flat side of a second cookie against the filling, as if making a sandwich. Press gently just until the filling is at the edge of the cookies. Roll the filled edge in chopped pistachios. Repeat until all the cookies form sandwiches.

When he's not working, Scott Rohr of St. Paul, Minnesota, is baking. "It's sort of a joke with my friends," he said. "I don't remember a time when I haven't baked. I grew up in one of those houses where everything was homemade. Some people come home from work and boil water for dinner. I take out eggs and butter." For his winning recipe, Rohr started with his tattered recipe card for a cream-of-tartar-based sugar cookie, which is a copy of a similarly well-worn card from his grandmother's kitchen. The filling and the pistachios, however, were all his idea. "I just started messing around," he said. "It's really hard for me to follow a recipe. These cookies aren't complicated, and they come together fast. They look like something substantial, but they're not hard to make. If you've ever baked a cookie, then you can bake these, for heaven's sake."

SAMBUCA CHOCOLATE CRINKLES

MAKES ABOUT 4 DOZEN COOKIES

Note: This dough must be prepared in advance.

12 ounces bittersweet chocolate	1 cup granulated sugar, divided
1 tablespoon unsalted butter	1 cup raw almonds, finely chopped
3 eggs	2/3 cup flour
2 tablespoons Sambuca Black (an anise-flavored liqueur)	3/4 teaspoon baking soda
	1/3 cup powdered sugar

In a double boiler over gently simmering water (or in a bowl in a microwave oven), melt the chocolate and butter, stirring to combine. Remove the chocolate mixture from the heat and cool slightly.

In a large bowl, whisk together the eggs, Sambuca Black, and ½ cup granulated sugar. Add the chocolate mixture and whisk until combined. Fold in the almonds, flour, and baking soda until combined; the dough will be soft and sticky. Cover the bowl with plastic wrap and refrigerate for at least 4 hours or up to 24 hours.

When ready to bake, preheat the oven to 350°F and line the baking sheets with parchment paper. In a small bowl, combine the remaining ½ cup granulated sugar and powdered sugar. With slightly wet fingers, shape teaspoon-size balls of dough. Roll them in the sugar mixture and place 2 inches apart on the prepared baking sheets. Bake until the cookies are puffed, cracked, and just set, 10 to 12 minutes. Remove the cookies from the oven and cool completely on the baking sheets.

Robert Bantle of St. Paul, Minnesota, is a serious baker. "If I don't have at least ten pounds of flour in the house, I feel like something bad could happen," he said with a laugh. That explains why he buys the staple in twenty-five-pound quantities. And lots of chocolate: boxes with names such as Scharffen Berger, Valrhona, Guittard, and Ghirardelli line the pantry in his kitchen. Not that he eats it. "I never crave chocolate," Bantle said. "Or sweets. I'd rather eat a bag of Doritos. So it's hard to know why I like these cookies. Maybe it's that dark bittersweet chocolate, or maybe it's the surprise of the Sambuca's anise flavor." Or it could be the texture. "They have a really nice crunch on the outside," he said, which he believes is the result of allowing the cookies to cool completely on baking sheets. "But inside they're tender and moist, like a brownie."

STRAWBERRY MARGARITA GEMS

MAKES 3 TO 4 DOZEN COOKIES

Note: This recipe must be prepared in advance. Strawberry jam can be substituted for the strawberry filling. Just add 1 teaspoon freshly grated lime zest to 1 cup jam.

For strawberry filling:

1 pound frozen strawberries, thawed and chopped

1 cup granulated sugar

1 teaspoon freshly squeezed lime juice

For cookies:

2¼ cups plus 2 tablespoons flour

1 teaspoon baking powder

¼ teaspoon salt

1 cup (2 sticks) unsalted butter, at room temperature

⅔ cup granulated sugar, plus extra for rolling dough

2 egg yolks

Freshly grated zest from 1 lime

2 teaspoons freshly squeezed lime juice

Flaky sea salt or coarse kosher salt, for decorating

To prepare strawberry filling: In a saucepan over medium heat, combine the strawberries and granulated sugar, and cook until the mixture is reduced to 1 cup. Remove the berry mixture from the heat, cool slightly, and stir in the lime juice. Transfer the mixture to a small bowl, cover with plastic wrap, and refrigerate overnight.

To prepare cookies: Preheat the oven to 350°F and line the baking sheets with parchment paper. In a large bowl, whisk together the flour, baking powder, and salt, and reserve. In a bowl of an electric mixer on medium-high speed, beat the butter until creamy, about 1 minute. Add the granulated sugar and beat until light and fluffy, about 2 minutes. Add the egg yolks, one at a time, beating well after each addition. Add the lime zest and lime juice, and beat until thoroughly combined. Reduce the speed to low and add the flour mixture, in thirds, mixing until combined. Shape the dough into ¾-inch balls. Roll the dough in granulated sugar and place 1 inch apart on the prepared baking sheets. Using your finger or a ½-teaspoon measuring spoon, make a deep indentation in each cookie, pressing together any cracks that may form. Fill indentations with the strawberry filling (you will not use all the filling).

Bake until the cookies are golden brown on the bottom, 16 to 18 minutes. Remove the cookies from the oven and cool for 2 minutes before transferring them to a wire rack to cool completely. Top each cookie with a few grains of sea salt or kosher salt.

"I'm a huge Food Network junkie," said Lance Swanson of North Branch, Minnesota. "I was watching Emeril make thumbprint cookies with raspberries and lemon zest, and I thought, 'That's wonderful, but what could I do different?' I like margaritas, so I thought, 'Strawberry and lime, they go together.' From there, I putzed around until I found something that I liked." Swanson doesn't use a jarred jam in this recipe—that's his baking-from-scratch ethos at work. "I started helping my mom in the kitchen when I was a little kid," he said. "Ever since I can remember I was helping my mom measure out flour, picking up tips and tricks. I like to challenge myself in the kitchen, give myself a goal. It's an excuse to experiment and a labor of love."

Surprisingly few people have asked Dianne Kemp of Chanhassen, Minnesota, to share her recipe for Swiss Chocolate Buttersweets. Kemp theorizes that folks are put off by their baked-by-a-pro appearance. "They're not difficult to make, but they give the impression that they are," she said. This cheesecake-like cookie may not exactly shout "Deck the Halls," but a single taste reveals a highly appropriate level of celebratory overkill. "They're not the typical Christmas cookie, but they're decadent and creamy," she said, although she makes them only in December. "I figure I should make people wait," she said, "and really want them."

SWISS CHOCOLATE BUTTERSWEETS
MAKES ABOUT 4 DOZEN COOKIES

For filling:

8 ounces cream cheese, at room temperature

1 cup powdered sugar

¼ cup flour

1½ teaspoons vanilla extract

1 cup chopped walnuts, optional

½ cup coconut

For cookies:

2¼ cups flour

¼ teaspoon salt

1 cup (2 sticks) unsalted butter, at room temperature

1 cup powdered sugar

2 teaspoons vanilla extract

For frosting:

1 cup milk chocolate or semisweet chocolate chips

4 tablespoons (½ stick) unsalted butter

2 tablespoons water

1 tablespoon white corn syrup

1½ cups powdered sugar

1 cup chopped walnuts, optional

½ cup coconut

To prepare filling: In a bowl of an electric mixer on medium-high speed, beat the cream cheese until creamy, about 1 minute. Gradually add the powdered sugar and beat until light and fluffy, about 2 minutes. Add the vanilla extract and beat until thoroughly combined. Reduce the speed to low, add the flour, and mix until just combined. Stir in the nuts, if using, and coconut, and reserve.

To prepare cookies: Preheat the oven to 350°F and line the baking sheets with parchment paper. In a medium bowl, whisk together the flour and salt, and reserve. In a bowl of an electric mixer on medium-high speed, beat the butter until creamy, about 1 minute. Gradually add the powdered sugar and beat until light and fluffy, about 2 minutes. Add the vanilla extract and beat until thoroughly combined. Reduce the speed to low, add the flour mixture, and mix until just combined. Shape teaspoons of dough into balls, place 2 inches apart on the prepared baking sheets, and make an indentation in the center of each cookie with your thumb.

Bake until very lightly browned, 12 to 15 minutes. Remove the cookies from the oven and cool for 2 minutes before transferring them to a wire rack. While the cookies are still warm, fill the indentations with the cream cheese mixture. Cool cookies completely.

To prepare frosting: In a double boiler over gently simmering water (or in a bowl in a microwave oven), melt the chocolate chips and butter. Stir in water and corn syrup. Add the powdered sugar and whisk until smooth. Frost each cookie.

TAFFY TREATS

MAKES ABOUT 3 DOZEN COOKIES

For filling:

1⅓ cups walnuts, divided	⅓ cup evaporated milk
⅓ cup granulated sugar	

For cookies:

½ cup (1 stick) unsalted butter, at room temperature	¼ teaspoon salt
	1 egg
¼ cup firmly packed brown sugar	1 teaspoon vanilla extract
¼ cup powdered sugar	2 cups flour
	Round, colored toothpicks

For caramel coating:

1 (14-ounce) package caramels, unwrapped	⅔ cup evaporated milk

To prepare filling: In a food processor fitted with a metal blade, pulse the walnuts until finely chopped. In a small saucepan over medium heat, combine ⅓ cup of the ground walnuts (reserve the remaining walnuts), granulated sugar, and ⅓ cup evaporated milk, and cook, stirring constantly, until very thick, about 5 minutes. Remove the pan from the heat, cool, and reserve.

To prepare cookies: Preheat the oven to 350°F and line the baking sheets with parchment paper. In a bowl of an electric mixer on medium-high speed, beat the butter until creamy, about 1 minute. Add the brown sugar, powdered sugar, and salt and beat until light and fluffy, about 2 minutes. Add the egg and vanilla extract, and beat until thoroughly combined. Reduce the speed to low, add the flour, and mix until just combined.

Shape the dough into 1-inch balls. Make a depression in each ball with your thumb and spoon ¼ teaspoon filling into the depression. Reshape the cookie into a ball, enclosing the filling. Place the cookies 2 inches apart on the prepared baking sheets and bake 15 to 18 minutes, or until lightly browned. Remove the cookies from the oven and cool for 2 minutes before transferring them to a wire rack. Insert a rounded, colored wooden toothpick into the top of each cookie and cool completely.

To prepare caramel coating: In a double boiler over gently simmering water (or in a bowl in a microwave oven), combine the caramels and ⅔ cup evaporated milk. Heat until the caramels melt, stirring occasionally; if too thick, thin with water, 1 tablespoon at a time. (If using a microwave oven, melt the caramels in 1-minute intervals, stirring and repeating until all of the caramel is melted.) Remove the pan from the heat but keep the mixture warm over hot water. Dip the cooled cookies into the caramel coating, allowing the excess caramel to drop off (the cookies can be double-dipped). Dip the bottom of the cookie in the remaining 1 cup ground walnuts and place on wax or parchment paper to set.

Sherryl Joos of Plymouth, Minnesota, described her first-place cookies to a T. "They grab the eye," she said. "People always say, 'Wow!' And they taste so good." She was right: The cookies grabbed the judges' eyes. And taste buds. Members of her family refer to the walnut–caramel treat as the "Toothpick Cookies," but Joos felt the familiar name had a low-wattage marquee value, so she improvised. But whatever Joos calls them, they're terrific and a staple of her holiday baking routine. In December, when she bakes ten dozen of her favorite cookie—inspired, at least in the looks department, by the candied apple—Joos will steer some into cookie exchanges and others into boxes for lucky recipients on her gift list. "A lot of friends get mad at me if I don't make them," she said. "They take a long time. But they're worth it."

Bar
COOKIES

A lemon ricotta cookie encountered at a favorite restaurant sparked the imagination of Karen Cope of Minneapolis, Minnesota. She test-drove a few versions and liked them well enough, but ultimately decided to streamline the process by going the bar cookie route, adding an icing (her favorite cream cheese–based frosting) and then playing with flavors. "I love almond, and I always have almond extract on hand," she said. "The recipe has the equivalent of a tablespoon of almond extract, and I was a little nervous about putting too much almond in. But then a friend didn't think it was almondy enough." It is.

ALMOND RICOTTA BARS

MAKES ABOUT 4 DOZEN BAR COOKIES

Note: To toast almonds, place the nuts in a dry skillet over medium heat and cook, stirring or shaking the pan frequently, until they just begin to release their fragrance, about 3 to 4 minutes (alternately, preheat the oven to 325°F, spread the nuts on an ungreased baking sheet, and bake, stirring often, for 4 to 6 minutes). Remove the nuts from the heat and cool to room temperature. For the best flavor, avoiding substitutions with this recipe—use whole milk ricotta, not low-fat. For more cake-like bars, use a 9- by 13-inch pan.

For bars:

2½ **cups flour**	2 **cups granulated sugar**
1 **tablespoon baking powder**	2 **eggs**
1 **teaspoon salt**	2 **teaspoons almond extract**
1 **cup (2 sticks) unsalted butter,**	1 **teaspoon vanilla extract**
at room temperature, plus extra for pan	1 **(15-ounce) container whole-milk ricotta cheese**

For frosting:

½ **cup (1 stick) unsalted butter,**	3 **cups powdered sugar**
at room temperature	1 **teaspoon almond extract**
4 **ounces cream cheese,**	½ **cup sliced almonds, toasted**
at room temperature	

To prepare bars: Preheat the oven to 325°F. Butter the bottom and sides of a 13- by 18-inch half-sheet pan. In a medium bowl, sift together the flour, baking powder, and salt, and reserve.

In a bowl of an electric mixer on medium-high speed, beat the butter until creamy, about 1 minute. Add the granulated sugar and beat until light and fluffy, about 2 minutes. Add the eggs, one at a time, and beat until thoroughly combined. Add the almond extract and vanilla extract, and beat until thoroughly combined. Reduce the speed to low and add the ricotta, a third at a time, and mix until just combined. Gradually add the flour mixture and mix until just combined.

Spread the batter in the prepared pan and bake until the cake is set, lightly golden, and the edges are starting to pull away from the sides of the pan, about 35 to 45 minutes. Remove the pan from the oven and place it on a wire rack to cool completely.

To prepare frosting: In a bowl of an electric mixer on medium-high speed, beat the butter and cream cheese until light and fluffy, about 2 minutes. Reduce the speed to low, add the powdered sugar and almond extract, and beat until the mixture is uniform and creamy. Spread the frosting over the cooled bar cookies, slice into squares, and top squares with toasted almonds.

ALMOND TRIANGLES
MAKES 4 TO 6 DOZEN BAR COOKIES

Note: This dough must be prepared in advance. These bar cookies freeze really well.

2 cups (4 sticks) unsalted butter,
at room temperature, divided

¾ cup granulated sugar, divided

1 egg

¾ teaspoon almond extract

½ teaspoon salt

2¾ cups flour

1 cup packed brown sugar

⅓ cup honey

¼ cup heavy cream

1 pound (about 5 ¼ cups) sliced almonds

Carefully line a 10- by 15-inch jelly roll pan with aluminum foil, shiny side up. In a bowl of an electric mixer on medium-high speed, beat 1 cup butter until creamy, about 1 minute. Gradually add ½ cup granulated sugar and beat until light and fluffy, about 2 minutes. Add the egg, almond extract, and salt, and beat until thoroughly combined. Reduce the speed to low, add the flour, and mix until just combined. Press the dough evenly into the pan and push dough up the sides. Cover the bowl with plastic wrap and refrigerate for 30 minutes.

When ready to bake, preheat the oven to 375°F. Using a fork, prick the dough in 20 to 24 places all across the dough and bake 10 minutes. Remove the pan from the oven and place it on a wire rack to cool.

In a large saucepan over medium heat, combine the brown sugar, honey, remaining 1 cup of butter, and remaining ¼ cup granulated sugar, and cook, stirring occasionally, until the sugar dissolves. Increase the heat to medium-high, bring the mixture to a boil, and cook for 3 minutes without stirring. Remove the pan from the heat and stir in the cream. Stir in the almonds. Spread the almond mixture evenly over the crust. Return the pan to the oven and bake until bubbling, about 15 minutes. Remove the pan from the oven and place on a wire rack to cool. While bars are still slightly warm, cut into triangles.

When a recipe requires four sticks of butter and five cups of almonds, can there possibly be a downside? Turns out the answer is "No." Charlotte Midthun of Granite Falls, Minnesota, encountered this recipe in *First for Women* magazine and had a hunch it would be a hit. "I took them to a party, and everyone loved them," she said. "I've been making them ever since. They're such a nice contrast to all the chocolate cookies and sugar cookies you see at Christmas." They sure are.

CARDAMOM SHORTBREAD COOKIES

MAKES ABOUT 3 DOZEN BAR COOKIES

Note: These take a long time in the oven—an hour, at a low temperature. But the prep time is easy.

For cookies:

2 cups flour	½ cup granulated sugar
2 teaspoons ground cardamom	½ cup light brown sugar
¼ teaspoon salt	1 egg, separated
1 cup (2 sticks) unsalted butter, at room temperature	1 teaspoon vanilla extract
	⅓ cup chopped nuts

For icing:

1½ tablespoons unsalted butter, melted	Milk as needed
½ teaspoon vanilla extract	Candied fruit for garnish, optional
1 cup powdered sugar	

To prepare cookies: Preheat the oven to 275°F. (Yes, this temperature is correct.) In a medium bowl, whisk together the flour, cardamom, and salt, and reserve.

In a bowl of an electric mixer on medium-high speed, beat the butter until creamy, about 1 minute. Add the granulated sugar and brown sugar, and beat until light and fluffy, about 2 minutes. Add the egg yolk and vanilla extract, and beat until thoroughly combined. Reduce the speed to low, add the flour mixture, and mix until just combined. Spread the dough into an ungreased 9- by 13-inch baking pan. Brush the egg white over the dough, sprinkle evenly with chopped nuts, and bake for 1 hour. Remove the pan from the oven and place on a wire rack to cool.

To prepare icing: In a bowl of an electric mixer on medium speed, beat the melted butter, vanilla extract, and powdered sugar until creamy, about 2 minutes. Add the milk, 1 teaspoon at a time, until the icing reaches drizzling consistency. Spread the icing on the slightly warm bars and garnish with candied fruit, if desired. Allow the icing to set and cut the bars while they are still slightly warm.

The sorry state of Alecia Enger's recipe card for her Cardamom Shortbread Cookies—stained, splattered, and smudged—is a testament to their popularity. Enger conjured up the bar cookie nearly twenty years ago, a response to her mother's love of shortbread and Enger's dislike of fussy shortbread molds. "I was pressed for time," said the Hudson, Wisconsin, resident. "So instead of using a mold, I just pressed the dough into a 9- by 13-inch pan." She has made them more times than she can count—with good reason. Not only do they make a lasting impression on eaters, but they are a snap in the kitchen, and the cardamom is a nod to Enger's Scandinavian ancestry.

KIT KAT CHRISTMAS BARS
MAKES ABOUT 3 DOZEN BAR COOKIES

Note: Decorate with dry-roasted, unsalted peanuts to make obvious to those with food allergies that these bar cookies contain peanuts. Natural peanut butter (no sugar added) really works well for these cookies. These bar cookies don't require an oven, the only no-bake recipe featured in our contest.

- 1 cup (2 sticks) unsalted butter
- ½ cup milk
- ⅓ cup granulated sugar
- 1 cup packed brown sugar
- 2 cups crushed graham crackers
- 1 (13.7 ounces) box Keebler Club Crackers
- ½ cup semisweet chocolate chips
- ½ cup butterscotch chips
- ⅓ cup peanut butter
- Decorative sugars and/or chopped dry-roasted, unsalted peanuts, optional

In a saucepan over medium heat, combine the butter, milk, granulated sugar, brown sugar, and graham crackers. Bring to a boil and stir continuously for 5 minutes; do not allow the mixture to burn. Remove the pan from the heat.

Line the bottom of a 9- by 13-inch pan with a single layer of Club Crackers. Pour half of the graham cracker mixture over the Club Crackers. Add a second layer of Club Crackers over the mixture. Pour the remaining half of the graham cracker mixture over the second layer of Club Crackers. Add a third layer of Club Crackers. Cover the pan with plastic wrap and refrigerate until set.

When the bars are set, combine the chocolate chips, butterscotch chips, and peanut butter in a double boiler over gently simmering water (or in a bowl in a microwave oven), stirring occasionally until the mixture is fully melted and smooth. Pour the melted topping over the top layer of Club Crackers and spread evenly across the bars. Sprinkle with chopped peanuts or decorative sugars, if desired. Allow the chocolate topping to cool. Cut into squares and serve.

"It's a super-stupid recipe, but I mean that in the nicest possible way," said Julie Olson of East Bethel, Minnesota. "I love cooking. I can cook like nobody's business. But I'm not a baker. But even if you're not a baker, you can make them, because they're so incredibly easy to make." Olson gleaned the recipe from her mother-in-law ("It was a collaboration between us," she said), and she's been making the recipe "for forever." Although she prepares Kit Kat Christmas Bars year-round, during the holidays Olson makes them extra-special. "I try to make them festive looking," she said. "Sugars, or sprinkles, or other decorations. You can make it however you want."

KOSSUTH KIFLI

MAKES 2 TO 3 DOZEN BAR COOKIES

2 teaspoons baking powder	8 eggs, separated
1²/₃ cups flour, plus extra for pan	½ teaspoon vanilla
1 cup (2 sticks) unsalted butter, at room temperature, plus extra for pan	Freshly grated peel and juice of 1 lemon
1½ cups granulated sugar	1½ cups finely chopped walnuts
	Powdered sugar for garnish

Preheat the oven to 350°F. Butter and flour the bottom and sides of a 9- by 13-inch cake pan. In a medium bowl, whisk together the baking powder and flour, and reserve.

In a bowl of an electric mixer on medium-high speed, beat the butter until creamy, about 1 minute. Add the granulated sugar and beat until light and fluffy, about 2 minutes. Add the egg yolks, one at a time, and beat until creamy. Add the vanilla extract, lemon rind, and lemon juice, and beat until thoroughly combined. Reduce the speed to low, gradually add the flour mixture, and mix until just combined.

In a bowl of an electric mixer on high speed, beat the egg whites until stiff but not dry. Using a spatula, fold the egg whites into the batter. Gently spread the batter into the prepared pan. Evenly sprinkle the top of the batter with walnuts and bake 25 to 30 minutes. Remove the pan from the oven and place on a wire rack to cool.

Cool until the cake shrinks away from the sides of the pan, about 15 minutes. With a small round biscuit cutter periodically dipped in powdered sugar, cut one circle (don't remove it), then cut another circle halfway down the first one, making two crescents and one oval scrap. Remove from pan and repeat. Cool crescents completely and dust with powdered sugar shaken through a wire-mesh screen. Store in a tightly covered container for up to 2 days.

The lemon-infused, walnut-topped, crescent-shaped Kossuth Kifli (pronounced coo-SOOTH KEY-flee) may be the only cookie bearing a general's name. Honoring historical figures with a cookie christening is a time-honored Hungarian tradition, said Linda Paul of Minneapolis, Minnesota. These cutouts (kifli is Hungarian for crescent) are a tribute to General Louis Kossuth, a nineteenth-century Hungarian revolutionary hero. Paul's entry originated with her mother's Hungarian church social group cookbook in Detroit. "Most of the recipes listed the ingredients but offered no instructions," Paul said with a laugh. But that culinary roadblock didn't stop this avid baker, and Kossuth Kifli have been at the heart of her holiday baking repertoire for several decades. "People love them," Paul said. "Maybe it's because they look a heck of a lot more difficult to make than they really are."

Other
COOKIES

ALMOND SPOONS
MAKES ABOUT 2 DOZEN COOKIES

Note: Vanilla sugar is available in some supermarkets and specialty food stores. Or make your own by splitting 1 vanilla bean, burying it into ½ pound of granulated sugar, and storing it in a tightly sealed container for 1 week. If you prefer, skip the shaping of the cookie. They also look pretty in their wafer-like appearance straight from the oven.

7 tablespoons unsalted butter	¼ teaspoon vanilla sugar
1 scant cup finely chopped almonds	1 tablespoon heavy whipping cream
1 cup granulated sugar	1 tablespoon half-and-half
1 tablespoon flour	1 tablespoon light corn syrup

Preheat the oven to 375°F and line the baking sheets with parchment paper. In a double boiler over gently simmering water (or in a bowl in a microwave oven), melt the butter and then slightly cool.

In a large bowl, combine the melted butter, almonds, granulated sugar, flour, vanilla sugar, cream, half-and-half, and corn syrup, and mix thoroughly. Drop teaspoons of the dough on the prepared baking sheets, spacing cookies 3 inches apart and baking 4 to 6 cookies at a time. (The cookies spread greatly.) Bake until lightly golden brown, about 8 minutes. Remove the cookies from the oven.

Carefully slide the parchment paper off the baking sheet onto a flat work surface. Using a thin metal spatula, lift the cookies off the parchment paper and, with your hand, gently bend the flat cookie into the shape of a taco shell (the "spoon" of its name). If you prefer, you can drape plastic wrap over a broomstick-size dowel and drape the cookie over it to create the "spoon" shape; cool completely. The shaping takes some practice; the cookies need to be cool enough to hold their shape, but not so cool that they have set and hardened. If the cookies have become too cool, return the parchment paper to the hot baking sheet to warm up the cookies.

"All of my recipes are from my childhood," said Sharon Severson of North Oaks, Minnesota. "I have boxes of my mom's old recipes and a file of some of the favorites that I make regularly. This is something she called 'Almond Lace.' She would spool them around the krumkake iron, but I just drape them over a dowel, like a taco shell. They're very pretty on a plate; they're almost like candy." Severson grew up on a farm on the Iron Range, the second-youngest of her Swedish immigrant parents' ten children. "I liked being in the kitchen with my mom," she said. "She was a fantastic cook and baker. We lived off the land. My two daughters laugh when I tell them stories about growing up on the farm. They say I'm like Laura Ingalls in *Little House in the Big Woods*. I'm a city girl now, but you can't take the country out of me."

CHOCOLATE-DRIZZLED CHURROS

MAKES 5 TO 6 DOZEN COOKIES

Note: A recommended chocolate is Abuelita chocolate tablets, which are available at most Mexican supermarkets and specialty stores. Although you can use semi-sweet chocolate for this recipe, the Mexican chocolate brings the cookie to another level, giving it that extra spice, that extra authentic flavor.

½ cup plus ⅔ cup granulated sugar, divided

2½ teaspoons ground cinnamon, divided

2½ cups flour

¼ teaspoon salt

1 cup (2 sticks) unsalted butter, at room temperature

3 egg yolks, at room temperature

1½ teaspoons vanilla extract

3.15 ounces Mexican chocolate or semisweet chocolate, chopped

1 tablespoon heavy cream or half-and-half

Preheat the oven to 400°F and line the baking sheets with parchment paper. In a small bowl, combine ½ cup granulated sugar and 1½ teaspoons cinnamon, and reserve. In a medium bowl, whisk together the flour, salt, and remaining 1 teaspoon cinnamon, and reserve.

In a bowl of an electric mixer on medium speed, beat the butter until creamy, about 1 minute. Add the remaining ⅔ cup granulated sugar and beat until light and fluffy, about 2 minutes. Add the egg yolks and vanilla extract, and beat until thoroughly combined. Reduce the speed to low, add the flour mixture, and mix until just combined. Transfer the dough to a pastry bag (or cookie press) fitted with a star or ribbon die, and pipe 3-inch long sticks, 1 inch apart, on the prepared baking sheets.

Bake until lightly browned, 9 to 11 minutes. Remove the cookies from the oven and cool for 2 minutes before transferring them to a wire rack until they are cool to the touch. Carefully dredge the cookies in the sugar–cinnamon mixture and return them to a wire rack to cool completely.

In a double boiler over gently simmering water (or in a bowl in a microwave oven), melt the chocolate and cream (or half-and-half), stirring occasionally until the chocolate is melted and smooth (if using Mexican chocolate, the mixture will be grainy). Transfer the chocolate to a pastry bag fitted with a small plain tip (or a plastic sandwich bag with one corner removed with a small cut). Drizzle the chocolate over each cookie. Allow the chocolate to set before serving.

The idea of creating a cookie version of the churro, the sweet fried-dough snack, occurred to Lance Swanson of North Branch, Minnesota, while he was shopping. "We go to Costco a lot, and I'll buy churros once in a while," he said. "I was eating them and started thinking, 'This would be a good cookie.' I started looking at spritz cookie recipes, and then it was a matter of tweaking the flavors. This is what I came up with." Judges were impressed. "They really capture the churro-ness of churros," said one judge. "This would be a fun State Fair food," said another. Swanson encourages bakers to seek out Mexican chocolate. "It's not like I'm going to invade your kitchen and start yelling at you if you don't," he said with a laugh.

"To me, this cookie just looks like the holidays," said Mary Martin of Minneapolis, Minnesota. "It's the cranberries, and the rosemary, and the orange glaze. Baking is a gift to your company. You put a little love into it." Martin's affection for cornmeal—the cookie's secret weapon—is based on the happy memories of her Virginia grandmother's kitchen. "My baking roots come from her," she said. "Cornmeal is the South, and Southerners like cornbread. For as long as I can remember, my grandmother would make cornbread. She'd crumple it up and add milk and sugar, and it was wonderful."

CRANBERRY CORNMEAL SHORTBREAD COOKIES

MAKES ABOUT 2½ DOZEN (2-INCH RECTANGLE) COOKIES

Note: This dough must be prepared in advance. Use more or less rosemary and dried cranberries, according to your preferences. If you prefer not to bother with cookie cutters, simply form the dough into a ball (do not refrigerate), shape it into a flat 8-inch circle on the prepared baking sheet, and score into 16 wedges. Poke each wedge at least twice with a fork. Bake as directed; then rescore the cookies, cool, and glaze.

For glaze:

⅓ cup powdered sugar	2 to 4 teaspoons freshly squeezed orange juice
1 teaspoon freshly grated orange zest	

For cookies:

1 cup flour, plus extra for rolling dough	Pinch of cayenne pepper
¼ cup finely ground yellow cornmeal	½ cup (1 stick) unsalted butter, chilled and cut into small pieces
3 tablespoons granulated sugar	
1 to 2 teaspoons freshly chopped rosemary	2 to 4 tablespoons chopped dried cranberries

To prepare glaze: In a medium bowl, whisk together the powdered sugar, orange zest, and 2 teaspoons orange juice, adding more orange juice, a teaspoon at a time, until the glaze is slightly runny. Reserve.

To prepare cookies: In a large bowl, whisk together the flour, cornmeal, granulated sugar, rosemary, and cayenne. Using a pastry blender, cut in the butter until the mixture resembles coarse meal. (You may need to add water, ½ teaspoon at a time, to help the dough come together.) Stir in the dried cranberries. Form the dough into a disk, wrap in plastic wrap, and refrigerate for at least 1 hour.

When ready to bake, preheat the oven to 325°F and line the baking sheets with parchment paper. On a lightly floured surface using a lightly floured rolling pin, roll the dough to ¼-inch thickness. Use cookie cutters to cut the dough and place the cookies 2 inches apart on the prepared baking sheets. Repeat with the remaining dough, gathering up scraps, re-rolling, and cutting until all the dough is used.

Bake until lightly brown, 21 to 24 minutes. Remove the cookies from the oven and cool on the baking sheets for 5 minutes. Brush the cookies with the glaze; then transfer the cookies to a wire rack to cool completely.

CRANBERRY PUMPKIN-SEED BISCOTTI

MAKES ABOUT 2 DOZEN BISCOTTI

4½ cups flour
1 teaspoon baking soda
1 teaspoon baking powder
½ teaspoon salt
2 teaspoons slightly mashed fennel seeds
2 cups granulated sugar

4 tablespoons (½ stick) unsalted butter, melted and cooled
5 eggs, beaten
2 teaspoons vanilla extract
Freshly grated zest of 2 oranges
2 cups dried cranberries
2 cups raw pumpkin seeds (pepitas)

Preheat the oven to 350°F and line the baking sheets with parchment paper. In a large bowl, whisk together the flour, baking soda, baking powder, salt, and fennel seeds, and reserve.

In a bowl of an electric mixer on medium-high speed, beat the granulated sugar, melted butter, eggs, vanilla extract, and orange zest until thoroughly combined, about 2 minutes. Reduce the speed to low, add the flour mixture, and mix until just combined. Stir in the cranberries and pumpkin seeds.

Divide the dough into four equal parts and form each part into logs that are approximately 10 inches long and 2 inches in diameter. Transfer the logs to the prepared baking sheets and bake until golden brown and an inserted skewer comes out clean, about 25 to 30 minutes. Remove the logs from the oven and cool for 5 minutes. Transfer the baked logs to a cutting board and cut them diagonally into ½-inch thick slices.

Reduce the oven temperature to 325°F. Return the slices, cut-side up, to the prepared baking sheets and bake for about 5 minutes. Remove from the oven, turn the biscotti over, and bake an additional 5 minutes. Remove the cookies from the oven and cool for 2 minutes before transferring to a wire rack to cool completely.

Phyllis Kahn of Minneapolis, Minnesota, has a dozen variations in her biscotti repertoire. "This version, with its red and green, is especially for the holidays," she said. Her love affair with biscotti was born, in part, because of the cookie's sturdy practicality. "We have people scattered on both sides of the continent, so we usually end up going somewhere on the holidays," she said. "Transportable things are helpful." Kahn is no stranger to baking competitions, having once walked away with a first-place ribbon at the Minnesota State Fair. "And it was for something I don't even believe in, guiltless cheesecake," she said with a laugh. "I think I put biscotti into an ethnic baking category and got second or third. I'm naturally competitive. I don't enter if I can't win."

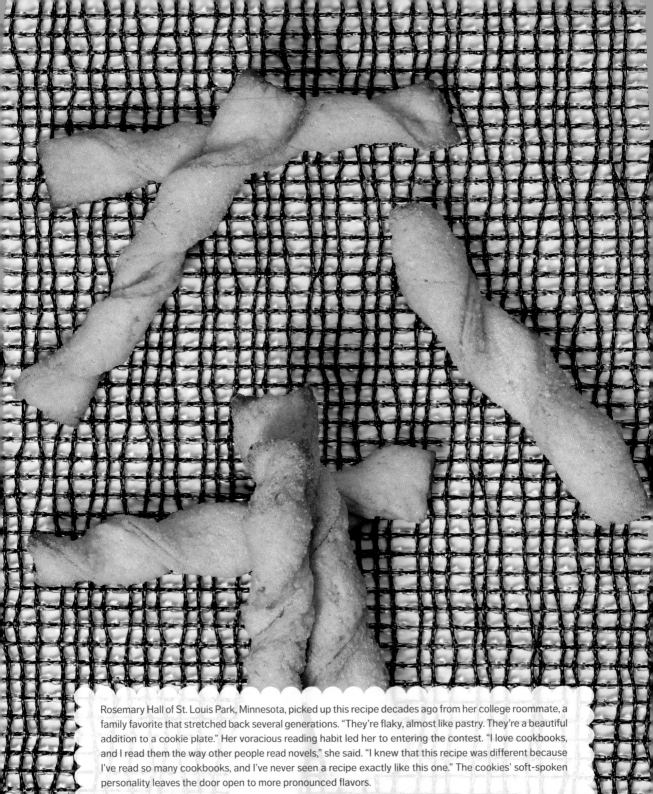

Rosemary Hall of St. Louis Park, Minnesota, picked up this recipe decades ago from her college roommate, a family favorite that stretched back several generations. "They're flaky, almost like pastry. They're a beautiful addition to a cookie plate." Her voracious reading habit led her to entering the contest. "I love cookbooks, and I read them the way other people read novels," she said. "I knew that this recipe was different because I've read so many cookbooks, and I've never seen a recipe exactly like this one." The cookies' soft-spoken personality leaves the door open to more pronounced flavors.

GERMAN SOUR CREAM TWISTS

MAKES ABOUT 5 DOZEN COOKIES

Note: This dough must be prepared in advance. The extra-large egg yolks make the dough easier to work with. Use flavored sugars, such as vanilla, cinnamon, or cardamom, for extra flavor, or add toasted finely ground nuts with the sugar. Adding chocolate is another possibility.

3½ cups flour	1 package (¼ ounce) dry yeast
1 teaspoon salt	¾ cup sour cream
½ cup shortening, chilled and cut into small pieces	1 extra-large egg plus 2 extra-large egg yolks, well beaten
½ cup (1 stick) unsalted butter, chilled and cut into small pieces	1 teaspoon vanilla extract
	1 cup sugar, divided

In a large bowl, whisk together the flour and salt. Using a pastry blender, cut in the shortening and butter until the mixture resembles coarse meal. In a small bowl, dissolve the yeast with 2 tablespoons warm water. Add the yeast mixture, sour cream, beaten eggs and egg yolks, and vanilla extract into the flour mixture, stirring until thoroughly combined. Cover the bowl with a damp cloth and refrigerate for 2 hours.

When ready to bake, preheat the oven to 375°F and line the baking sheets with parchment paper. Remove the bowl from the refrigerator and divide the dough in half, keeping the second portion refrigerated while preparing the first. Divide the sugar in half.

On a lightly sugared surface using a rolling pin, roll the dough to an 8- by 16-inch rectangle. Working quickly, fold one end in and fold the other end to cover, as with an envelope fold. Sprinkle with sugar. Flip the dough over and roll to the same 8- by 16-inch size. Fold again, sprinkle again, roll again. Repeat the process a third time.

Sprinkle more sugar over the rolled dough. Cut into 1- by 4-inch strips. Twist each strip, stretching the dough slightly. Repeat the process with the second half of dough and the remaining sugar.

Place twisted strips 2 inches apart on the prepared baking sheets and bake until lightly brown, about 10 to 12 minutes. Remove the cookies from the oven and cool for 2 minutes before transferring to a wire rack to cool completely.

MACADAMIA NUT TARTS

MAKES ABOUT 4 DOZEN COOKIES (MINI-MUFFIN SIZE)

Note: This dough must be prepared in advance. To prepare dried lemon peel, spread the zest of 1 large lemon on wax paper and allow to air-dry overnight. Try other nuts instead of macadamia, if you prefer. The cookie works in a variety of shapes, adapting to tart and mini-muffin pans of all sizes. Just remember it's a rich cookie, so smaller may be better in this case.

For crust:

3 **cups flour, plus extra for rolling dough**	1½ **cups (3 sticks) unsalted butter, at room**
½ **cup cornstarch**	**temperature, plus extra for tart pans**
½ **teaspoon salt**	⅔ **cup granulated sugar**
	Dried lemon zest from 1 large lemon

For topping:

10 **tablespoons (1 stick plus 2 tablespoons)**	⅓ **cup granulated sugar**
unsalted butter	2½ **tablespoons heavy cream**
½ **cup firmly packed brown sugar**	3 **cups macadamia nuts, coarsely chopped**

To prepare crust: Preheat the oven to 350°F and grease the mini-tart or mini-muffin pans. In a medium bowl, whisk together the flour, cornstarch, and salt, and reserve.

In a bowl of an electric mixer on medium-high speed, beat the butter until creamy, about 1 minute. Add the granulated sugar and lemon zest, and beat until light and fluffy, about 2 minutes. Reduce the speed to low, add the flour mixture, and mix just until the dough is crumbly.

On a lightly floured surface and using a lightly floured rolling pin, roll the dough to ⅜-inch thickness. Using a 2- or 3-inch biscuit cutter (depending on the size of mini-muffin pan or mini-tart pan), cut the dough and transfer dough rounds to the prepared pans, pressing into the pan and leaving a well in the center of each cookie (or form the dough into balls, press the dough into pans, and form the desired shape). Prick the dough with a fork and bake until light brown, about 16 to 18 minutes. Remove the pans from the oven and cool for 10 minutes. Then remove the cookies from the pans and place on a wire rack to cool completely.

To prepare topping: In a medium saucepan over medium heat, combine the butter, brown sugar, and granulated sugar. Stir constantly over medium heat until the mixture comes to a boil. Boil for 1 minute without stirring, until the mixture thickens and large bubbles begin to form. Remove the pan from the heat; stir in the nuts and cream. Spoon 1 to 2 tablespoons (depending on pan size) into each tart crust and cool completely.

Trish Cowle of Mendota Heights, Minnesota, adapted this recipe from one in *The Spirit of Christmas*. Along with graham cracker–chocolate rollouts, sugar cookies, and bars, Cowle's holiday baking schedule always includes Macadamia Nut Tarts. "I've been making them for twenty-three years," she said. "They get rave reviews. I have family members who insist on them." When she first came across the recipe, the main ingredient captured her attention. "I love macadamias and I thought, 'This has to be great,'" she said. "But then again, I love nuts."

To the best of her recollection, Kathie Nelson's signature Christmas cookie dates to the late 1960s, when a friend raved about a recipe she'd picked up from a utility company promotion. For Nelson, the details sounded just right. "My family loves the nutmeg and buttery rum flavors," she said. The Richfield, Minnesota, resident gave the cookie a shot but found that rolling and cutting dough was an activity too time-consuming for her baking tastes. So she improvised and reached for her cookie press. The impulse was a good one, and she's been making these eye-catching, spritz-inspired treats ever since.

NUTMEG STICKS
MAKES ABOUT 8 DOZEN COOKIES

For cookies:

3 **cups flour**	¾ **cup granulated sugar**
1 **teaspoon freshly grated nutmeg**	1 **egg**
¼ **teaspoon salt**	2 **teaspoons vanilla extract**
1 **cup (2 sticks) unsalted butter,**	2 **teaspoons rum flavoring**
at room temperature	**(or 1 to 2 tablespoons rum, to taste)**

For frosting:

⅓ **cup (5⅓ tablespoons) unsalted butter,**	2 **teaspoons rum flavoring**
at room temperature	**(or 1 to 2 tablespoons rum, to taste)**
2 **cups powdered sugar**	2 **tablespoons heavy cream**
2 **teaspoons vanilla extract**	**Freshly grated nutmeg for garnish**

To prepare cookies: Preheat the oven to 350°F and line the baking sheets with parchment paper. In a medium bowl, whisk together the flour, nutmeg, and salt, and reserve.

In a bowl of an electric mixer on medium-high speed, beat the butter until creamy, about 1 minute. Gradually add the granulated sugar and beat until light and fluffy, about 2 minutes. Add the egg and beat until thoroughly combined. Add the vanilla extract and rum flavoring, and beat until thoroughly combined. Reduce the speed to low, add the flour mixture, and mix until just combined.

Spoon the dough into a cookie press fitted with a small (⅝-inch) star plate. Holding the press in an almost horizontal position, form long rolls on the prepared baking sheets (rolls can be placed close together, as these cookies do not spread when baked). Cut the rolls into 3-inch sticks. Bake 10 minutes. Remove the cookies from the oven and allow them to cool completely on the baking sheets before transferring them to a wire rack.

To prepare frosting: In a bowl of an electric mixer on medium speed, beat the butter until creamy, about 1 minute. Gradually add the powdered sugar and beat until light and fluffy, about 2 minutes. Add the vanilla extract and rum flavoring, and beat until well combined. Add the cream and beat until the frosting is light and creamy. Frost each cookie and sprinkle with nutmeg.

RASPBERRY TRUFFLE TARTLETS

MAKES ABOUT 4 DOZEN COOKIES

Nonstick cooking spray

2½ cups flour

⅔ cup unsweetened cocoa powder

1 teaspoon baking soda

¼ teaspoon salt

1 cup (2 sticks) plus 2 tablespoons unsalted butter, at room temperature

¾ cup firmly packed brown sugar

⅔ cup granulated sugar

2 eggs

1 teaspoon vanilla extract

2½ tablespoons raspberry liqueur

1½ cups semisweet chocolate chips

8 ounces raspberry preserves

⅔ cup white chocolate chips

Preheat the oven to 350°F. Lightly coat mini-muffin tins with cooking spray.

In a medium bowl, whisk together the flour, cocoa, baking soda, and salt, and reserve.

In a bowl of an electric mixer on medium-high speed, beat the butter until creamy, about 1 minute. Add the brown sugar and granulated sugar, and beat until light and fluffy, about 2 minutes. Add the eggs, one at a time, beating well after each addition. Add the vanilla extract and raspberry liqueur, and beat until thoroughly combined. Reduce the speed to low, add the flour mixture, and mix until just combined. Stir in the semisweet chocolate chips.

Spoon the dough by heaping tablespoons and shape into balls. Place the balls into prepared mini-muffin tins and bake 7 minutes. Remove the tins from the oven and, using the back of a spoon, immediately (and gently) flatten the tops of the tartlets. Transfer the tins to a wire rack and cool for about 10 minutes. Using a thinly bladed knife, carefully separate the tartlets from the tin and remove. Transfer the tartlets to a wire rack to cool completely.

In a small bowl, stir the preserves. Place ½ teaspoon preserves on top of each tartlet and carefully spread.

In a double boiler over gently simmering water (or in a bowl in a microwave oven), melt the white chocolate chips, whisking occasionally. Using a spoon, drizzle the white chocolate over the tartlets.

Tricia Hall, a busy family physician in Minneapolis, Minnesota, self-medicates with baking. "It's sort of my therapy after a long day at work," she said. "I get home and I like to do something with my hands instead of my head. I'll often bake late at night and decompress that way." Chocolate and raspberry are two favorite tastes, so Hall used them as a starting point. A real "aha!" moment came when she added raspberry liqueur. Her nursing staff proved to be valuable taste-testers, and her mother-in-law added the final touch, a festive white chocolate drizzle. Her advice: savor them slowly. "They're not like a chocolate chip cookie," she said. "They're more like a truffle. You can get overloaded on the sugar high."

A self-described "Nordic food geek and meatball historian," Patrice Johnson of Roseville, Minnesota, stumbled on the basis for her winning formula in an "elderly but beloved" book from Time-Life's popular 1960s Foods of the World series. The recipe sparked a happy childhood memory. "My mom always made these little meringue cookies for Christmas," she said. "I loved them. I was the only one who ate them." Enriching meringue with cocoa came from a chocolate baking contest that Johnson entered, and the vinegar-infused chocolate filling grew out of a suggestion from a student in one of Johnson's cooking classes. "Easily the most beautiful cookie on the table," raved one judge, while others decreed "Wow" and "Gorgeous."

ROYAL SWEETS WITH CHOCOLATE–BALSAMIC SAUCE

MAKES ABOUT 2 DOZEN COOKIES

Note: Don't be afraid of piping the meringue into a cookie shape—it's not as difficult as it sounds!

For cookies:

- 4 egg whites, at room temperature
- ⅛ teaspoon cream of tartar
- Pinch of salt
- 1 cup superfine sugar
- 2 tablespoons unsweetened cocoa powder, sifted or whisked to remove lumps

For sauce:

- 3 ounces dark chocolate
- ⅓ cup heavy cream
- ¼ cup packed brown sugar
- 1 tablespoon balsamic vinegar
- 2 tablespoons unsalted butter, cold
- 1 teaspoon vanilla extract

To prepare cookies: Preheat the oven to 250°F and line the baking sheets with parchment paper. In a bowl of an electric mixer fitted with a whisk attachment on medium-high speed, beat the egg whites, cream of tartar, and salt until the mixture is foamy. Gradually add the superfine sugar and continue beating until the egg whites are very stiff and form solid peaks when the whisk is lifted out of the bowl, at least 5 minutes. Using a rubber spatula, carefully fold in the cocoa powder.

Using a pastry bag fitted with a star tip (or a plastic bag, with a corner cut out), fill the bag with batter and pipe a basket-shaped circular cookie, 1½ inches wide and 1½ inches tall, with a small indented opening in the center (or make a tiny depression in the top of the cookie with a wet finger or the back of a wet spoon). Alternately, use a small scoop to drop mounds of batter on the prepared baking sheets and make the indentation on top separately. Repeat with the remaining batter. Bake until the cookies are dry and crisp on the outside but tender on the inside, 50 to 60 minutes. If the cookies start to take on any color, reduce the heat to 200°F. Remove the pan from the oven and cool 5 minutes before transferring the cookies to a wire rack to cool completely.

To prepare sauce: In a small saucepan over low heat, combine the chocolate, cream, and brown sugar, stirring occasionally until the chocolate has melted. Stir in the vinegar. Remove the pan from the heat and stir in the butter until melted. Stir in the vanilla extract and cool slightly. Spoon the sauce into the center of the cookies.

ACKNOWLEDGMENTS

Our thanks go to the thousands of *Star Tribune* readers who have shared their recipes and stories every year. Without them, we would not have had a contest. Their involvement and interest—and, yes, excitement and exuberance—made this book possible. Thank you, thank you, thank you, about 3,500 times.

Thanks to our colleagues all over the *Star Tribune* newsroom for their years of baking (and judging) our semifinalists. Designer Nicole Hvidsten's inexhaustible skills year after year in the print edition of the *Star Tribune* merit special praise, as does her work, with Mike Rice, on earlier e-book editions of this recipe collection. Thanks also to designer Chrissy Ashack, who added her own spin to the print edition in recent years.

A special thanks to Amy Carter, formerly of Art Institutes International Minnesota, and the institute's fine folks (including students) for their generosity and baking skills. We appreciate the work of food stylist Carmen Bonilla, who prepared many of the cookies for photography (the less-than-perfect ones were baked by us).

We are grateful to the *Star Tribune* for its support of our Holiday Cookie Contest. No one flinched when we said, "Let's hold a contest." Not once in fifteen years.

A heartfelt thanks to the staff of the University of Minnesota Press, for bringing these cookies to a wider audience, and to editor Erik Anderson, who knew a winning recipe when he saw it.

And thanks to all those who love cookies! What could be a better treat? Bring on the flour, sugar, butter, and eggs. We have some work to do.

• • • •

We also have personal thanks to offer for our cookie-making skills.

Lee Svitak Dean: My mother, Laverne, kept the Svitak cookie jar overflowing with sugar cookies and gingersnaps; I never had a commercially made sweet until I begged for one so I could be like every other classmate. Christmas meant Norwegian treats, including sandbakkels, krumkake, and rosettes, with the guidance of my grandmother Martha Nelson, who also patiently supervised the baking and frosting of cutout cookies with her grandchildren. I do the same with my three grands today, cleaning up sprinkles for weeks.

Rick Nelson: I grew up surrounded by cookie-baking women, most of them of Scandinavian descent, including grandmothers Gay Olsen and Hedvig Nelson, great-aunts Alice Moe and Marian Moe, and aunts Millie Carlson, Marge Hermstad, Norrie Nelson, Jan Nelson, Elzina Nelson, Patricia Hoyt, Carolyn Brunelle, Mary Olsen, Susan Olsen, and Susan Nyhammer. My mother, Judy Nelson, instilled an everlasting love of Christmas—and Christmas cookies—into her kids, and I wish that I was as accomplished a Christmas cookie baker as my sister, Linda Korman. I'm grateful to my husband, Robert Davidian, for his support and for having the instinct to take only the ugly cookies off the test-batch tray.

COOKIES BY CATEGORY

International

COOKIES A–Z

COOKIES BY CONTEST YEAR

2003
Chocolate-Dipped Triple Coconut Haystacks, 20
Kossuth Kifli, 158
Swedish Shortbread Cookies, 69
Taffy Treats (winner), 146

2004
Alfajores (winner), 47
Cardamom Crescents, 102
Cashew Lemon Shortbread Cookies, 106
Cranberry-Filled Cookies, 59
Nutmeg Sticks, 175
Swiss Chocolate Buttersweets, 145

2005
Acorn Cookies, 94
Cardamom Shortbread Cookies, 155
Devil's Delight Cookies (winner), 24
Frosted Cashew Cookies, 28
Zazvorniky, 73

2006
Cranberry Cat Kisses, 113
Korova Cookies (winner), 85
Orange Kisses, 31
Pumpkin Cookies, 35
Sambuca Chocolate Crinkles, 141

2007
Almond Sandwiches, 48
Chai Crescents, 109
Grandma Eva's Ginger Cream Cookies, 60
Lime Coolers, 125
Orange Chocolate Cookies (winner), 66
Raspberry Truffle Tartlets, 176

2008
Almond Spoons, 163
Cardamom Cookies, 100
Cranberry Pumpkin-Seed Biscotti, 168
Double-Chocolate Espresso Cherry Drops
      (winner), 27
Ricotta Cheese Cookies, 39
Viennese Wafers with Lemon, 70

2009
Almond Triangles (winner), 152
Clare-oes, 56
French–Swiss Butter Cookies, 117
Kolaches, 63
Persian Molasses Crinkles, 137

2010
Hot and Sassy Peanut Butter Buds, 118
Nancy's Anise–Pecan Cookies, 86
Pistachio Orange Cookies (winner), 138
Red Velvet Whoopie Pies, 37
Strawberry Margarita Gems, 142

2011
Almond Palmiers, 77
Chocolate-Drizzled Churros, 164
Lemon–Lime Christmas Trees, 64
Snowball Clippers, 40
Swedish Almond Chocolate Macaroons (winner),
      43

2012
Cherry Almond Turnovers, 52
Cranberry Pecan Swirls, 83
Orange Ginger Drops, 134

COOKIES BY BAKER

Lee Svitak Dean is the longtime food editor at the *Star Tribune,* where she has guided the Taste section to multiple James Beard Awards, including one of her own, as well as an Emmy and recognition as "Best Food Section." She is the author of *Come One, Come All: Easy Entertaining with Seasonal Menus.*

Rick Nelson has been the *Star Tribune*'s restaurant critic and food writer since 1998. He is a James Beard Award winner, and his work has been published in four editions of the annual *Best Food Writing* anthologies, which present the best of American food journalism.

Tom Wallace had a long, award-winning career in small-town community journalism before he arrived at the *Star Tribune* in 1998 as a photographer and a photo editor. He uses those skills to showcase food at its best for the newspaper's Taste section and has won recognition for his work.